The Art of ARNOLD BENNETT

JAMES G. HEPBURN

The Art of

ARNOLD
BENNETT

Indiana University Press
Bloomington, 1963

To M

Contents

Acknowledgments

I OWE MY first debt to Professor T. E. M.
Boll, under whose direction I began studying Bennett. But
for his knowledge and encouragement, the present work
would not have been written. Secondly I am indebted
to my wife for many contributions to the substance of
my discussion. The book has also benefited from two very
thoughtful reviews of earlier stages of it by Professors
Maurice Beebe and Helmut E. Gerber. For other assistance
and suggestions I should like to thank Mr. George Beard-
more, Mr. G. J. V. Bemrose, Mrs. Dorothy Bennett, Mr.
Richard Bennett, Mr. Desmond Flower, Sir Newman
Flower, Mr. John Ford, Mr. W. W. Kennerley, Mr. Lionel
Lane, Mr. George McFarlane, Mr. Gilbert Miller, Mr. K.
D. Miller, Miss Winifred Nerney, Mr. Thomas R. Roberts,
Professor William M. Sale, Jr., and Mr. Frank Swinnerton.
I should like also to acknowledge an indirect indebtedness
to Professors Richard P. Adams, Robert H. Elias, Gordon
S. Haight, and Matthias Shaaber.

I am grateful for two grants-in-aid from the Department
of English of Cornell University that enabled me to do
some research in England. A small part of that work is
reflected in material in Chapter Eight and Appendix A.
I should also like to express my gratitude to the Faculty
Research Grants Committee of Cornell University for a
grant to pay for secretarial expenses in preparing the manuscript for publication.

I am obligated to several English and American publishers for permission to quote from Bennett's writings: the Bodley Head (*Don Juan de Marana*), Jonathan Cape (*Literary Taste*), Cassell (*Imperial Palace, Lord Raingo, Riceyman Steps*), Chatto & Windus (*Sacred and Profane Love*), Doubleday (*The Arnold Bennett Calendar, The Author's Craft, The Book of Carlotta, Clayhanger, The Glimpse, Imperial Palace, Literary Taste, Lord Raingo, A Man from the North, The Matador of the Five Towns, The Old Wives' Tale, The Pretty Lady, The Price of Love, Riceyman Steps, The Savor of Life, These Twain, Things That Have Interested Me, Second Series, Things That Have Interested Me, Third Series*), Hodder & Stoughton (publisher of *The Old Wives' Tale*), Methuen (*Clayhanger, A Man from the North, The Matador of the Five Towns, The Price of Love, These Twain*), and the Viking Press (*The Journal of Arnold Bennett*).

Mrs. Dorothy Bennett and the Library of University College, London, have kindly allowed me to quote from an unpublished letter from Bennett to J. B. Pinker. Mrs. Bennett and the New York Public Library, Henry W. and Albert A. Berg Collection, have allowed me to quote from unpublished letters from Bennett to George Sturt. To Mrs. Bennett I am also obliged for permission to quote from Bennett's journals and from two of his letters to her.

Other passages are quoted by permission of the following publishers: Edward Arnold and Harcourt, Brace & World (E. M. Forster's *Aspects of the Novel*), Harcourt, Brace & World and William Heinemann (Reginald Pound's *Arnold Bennett*), the Hogarth Press (Virginia Woolf's *Mr. Bennett and Mrs. Brown*), and Rupert Hart-Davis (*Hugh Walpole*). Most of Chapter Four is reprinted by permission from *Boston University Studies in English*, V (1961), 246-255.

Introduction

ARNOLD BENNETT's brief eminence as England's finest novelist of the early twentieth century and his longer eminence as one of her most powerful literary critics are dim facts of literary history. His descent was precipitous. When Virginia Woolf made her famous attack on his novels in 1924, she was delivering a long overdue *coup de grâce*. As she herself said, the world had changed about 1910, and Arnold Bennett had not recognized the fact. The reputation that he won in 1908 with *The Old Wives' Tale* was still bright in 1910, but by 1914 it was badly tarnished. Either date, though, 1910 or 1914, is the significant date in literary history to mark the end of an old world and the emergence of a new, and Bennett the novelist was going into eclipse then. The only valid reason for Mrs. Woolf's attack (she did not really intend to put the victim out of his misery) was that Bennett survived as a literary critic and expressed some reservations about her own work. Reputedly able to make or break a best-seller, he dominated book-reviewing in the twenties with his articles in the *Evening Standard*. For the great middle-brow reading public, his opinion was final. It was also ephemeral. With his death in 1931 it was forgotten. A reader today may be surprised to learn that in 1930 Bennett wrote of William Faulkner, " He has inexhaustible invention of powerful imagination, a wonderful gift of characterization, a fiendish skill in dialogue . . . ; Faulkner is the coming man "; that in 1922 he wrote of the

final chapter in *Ulysses,* " I doubt if I have ever read anything to equal it"; and that in 1913, when Henry James
was rating the young D. H. Lawrence much below Compton
Mackenzie, Bennett was recommending to the Stage Society
that it consider any play that Lawrence might write.

However reduced in stature Bennett may be as a novelist,
he is still to be reckoned with. If the literary historian is
concerned with the realist movement in English literature,
he must acknowledge Bennett as one of its most important
figures, perhaps its chief figure: a more genuine artist than
Galsworthy or Wells, a greater realist than Moore or
Gissing. If the historian is concerned with the novel since
1914, he must acknowledge origins: the specific indebtedness of Lawrence's *The Lost Girl* to Bennett's *Anna of the
Five Towns,* the more general indebtedness of Joyce's
Dublin to the towns and cities first delineated by the realists, the still broader indebtedness of fidelity in describing
the whole of life to the objectivity and truthfulness that
were the cornerstones of the realist tradition. If the historian
is concerned with literary value, as ultimately he must be,
he must ask whether the past forty years have afforded adequate light in which to judge Bennett. A few years ago
E. M. W. Tillyard reported he had rediscovered *The Old
Wives' Tale.* Over the course of years he had decided that
it was a minor work, and then on a rereading of it he
realized that it was a major work and deserved several
pages in his *The Epic Strain in the English Novel.* On the
same occasion he reread *Clayhanger* and decided that it
was indeed a minor work. Tillyard was the first important
critic in many years to speak highly of Bennett, and his
discussion of him is unusually valuable. But which of his
judgments will seem accurate forty years from now? The
task of replacing ephemeral judgments with permanent
ones is a continuing necessity.

Perhaps to reckon with any artist, especially in respect to values, is a task for an angel—a task that in the absence of angels human beings assume. The human hope is corrigibility, and thus the present study will attempt to shift the perspective in which Bennett is seen. In brief, the aim is to show that Bennett is not and did not consider himself to be primarily a realist whose main task was to describe the social scene; the aim is to show that he is equally a psychological realist, a symbolist, an allegorist, and—to use his own phrase—a discoverer of beauty. He will be shown to be as much a romantic as a realist.

These things may not seem surprising. They suggest, in part, the sort of paradox that is familiar in literary history: *Madame Bovary* serving as a model at once for prosaic realism and for artistry; realism and art-for-art's-sake flourishing together in the nineties. They may seem inevitably true to anyone who sees that all art is symbolic, that the artist pursues or avoids truth and reality by means of metaphors. Yet there is something surprising. For Bennett perhaps more than any other English realist has sometimes seemed to be a human photographic machine which recorded the facts of life that it focused upon: he may have possessed a philosophical outlook, but this was what gave him his camera eye, this turned his eye in one direction rather than another, this clicked the shutter when the events which served it had been adequately observed. To his more hostile critics, he has seemed in addition to be a businessman of letters, whose need to satisfy his audience occasionally obstructed his view.

It can be pointed out that simply as a realist Bennett has often been misunderstood. W. Y. Tindall, for example (writing in *Forces in Modern British Literature*), accuses Bennett of dishonesty in treating a social problem; he regards the ending of an early novel, *Leonora*, as a con-

cession to public taste rather than as a truthful conclusion
to a social scene: "He wanted a yacht." Two facts are
relevant: first, that *Leonora* is the middle book of a trilogy
whose other books end unhappily, one with the suicide of
the hero, the other with the accidental death of the heroine;
secondly—as Bennett explained in a letter to H. G. Wells—
that the ending of *Leonora* is only seemingly happy. The
heroine wins her man, but her unhappiness at the beginning of the novel is bound to reassert itself in events subsequent to the end; Leonora is momentarily happy, she is
self-deluded.

A problem of a similar sort arises with *The Old Wives'*
Tale. E. M. W. Tillyard sees the novel as a celebration of
provincial life, a "successful rendering of a choric feeling,
the feeling of provincial puritanism." Sophia Baines, for
example, who has abandoned home to follow the city-bred
Gerald Scales to London, forces her reluctant lover to marry
her. Bennett celebrates the provincial heritage that saves
her: "this fragile slip of the Baines stock, unconsciously
drawing upon the accumulated strength of generations of
honest living . . . , put a defeat upon him." Bennett means
what he says, but he means it in part ironically. For what
Sophia draws upon to save herself is equally some money
that she has just stolen from her aunt—money specifically
to enable her to act independently of Gerald. Bennett's
humor here is not more than a wink, if only because he
reckons Sophia's general conduct to be superior to Gerald's.
But a wink, no doubt. Moreover, Sophia's honest living,
illustrated with this theft (as well as with her later theft
from Gerald), leads to her miserliness in her years at the
Pension Frensham; and it leads ultimately, as does her
sister's, to an end in obscure death, celebrated by an old,
sick dog going to its meal.

The novel is as much as anything else a study in the

decay of values. The very symbol of mid-Victorian provincial values is Sophia's father, John Baines, whom the
reader sees only as a paralyzed old man, " far gone in decay
and corruption." When John Baines dies, " Mid-Victorian
England lay on that mahogany bed." There is other evidence in the novel that Bennett's celebration is ambiguous.
If external evidence were needed, one could point to some
of Bennett's privately expressed opinions. As a provincial
young man, he said to a friend in the Potteries—his Five
Towns, where he himself and the Baineses lived: " I'm
going to get out of this." He did, within a year, rarely to
return—as he wrote to his second wife—" except for funerals
and the bankruptcies of relatives." Once in later years
when he passed through the district in a train from Manchester, he wrote in his *Journal*: " the sight . . . gave me
a shudder."

Though there are elements of Bennett's realism that
remain to be clarified, the greater immediate task is to
explore the broader path that his art actually took. Three
comments by Bennett himself commend the task to the
critic. At the outset of his literary career he wrote that
" the day of my enthusiasm for ' realism,' for ' naturalism,'
has passed." He remarked on several occasions that " the
foundation of good fiction is character-creating, and nothing
else." And he reiterated again and again: " to find beauty,
which is always hidden—that is the aim." Moreover, in his
very first novel, he sought to achieve " a mosaic consisting
exclusively of Flaubert's *mots justes* " rather than the sociology of Balzac or Zola; from 1900 onward he set Dostoevsky
before him as the great literary figure to emulate; and he
was, in the experience of Ford Madox Ford, the only contemporary English novelist who loved to discuss literary
technique.

There has already been some examination of this other

Bennett. Among his major critics, Georges Lafourcade gives
attention to his psychological understanding; James Hall
discusses some aspects of structure in the novels; and Elizabeth Massoulard suggests Bennett's indebtedness to the
romantic tradition. But the first two investigations carry
modest weight in the works in which they appear, and the
third has received little attention. The present study extends these investigations. It hopes to show, by a close
examination of the novels, that Bennett is indeed more
interested in beauty than in realism, more interested in
character than in sociology, more interested in technique
than in undifferentiated facts of life. And some things
may be surprising. For Bennett's symbolism is not the
inevitable symbolism that Harry Levin describes in *Symbolism and Fiction*, the result of representing life by parts
and attributes; it is a deliberate and elaborate symbolism
that Bennett uses to disclose character and to discover
beauty.

Two recent dissertations on Bennett, by James G. Kennedy and Thomas J. Roberts, make significant contributions
to the study of this other Bennett. Although Mr. Kennedy
focuses upon Bennett's debt to Herbert Spencer, his analyses
of the structure and imagery of several of the novels reveal
the most conscious artistry. Mr. Roberts compares the techniques of Bennett's melodramas, farces, and realistic novels,
and explores the psychological bases and philosophical
perspectives of the three modes.

The present study makes no detailed attempt to place
Bennett in the literary tradition. To the extent that he is
a realist, that task has been performed elsewhere, most satis-
factorily by Lafourcade and Marilyn B. Saveson. To the
extent that he is not, this study aims only to offer an analysis
that will be useful in a general revaluation of the so-called
realistic novelists.

CHAPTER I

Realism vs. Character

THE OLD WIVES' TALE

WHEN DICKENS IN *Hard Times* describes Potteries workers at a strike meeting as " this crowd of earnest faces, whose honesty in the main no competent observer free from bias could doubt," possessing "great qualities, susceptible of being turned to the happiest and best account," he is guilty of that sentimental realism which is one of the hallmarks of Victorian fiction. When Bennett in *Hilda Lessways* describes another group of Potteries workers at a strike meeting as " ragged and shabby men . . . waiting to spring, like famished and ferocious tigers," he displays a realism that seems much nearer to the truth. Avid reader that he was, Bennett probably read *Hard Times* as well as *Germinal*, but it was Zola who moved him. He was reading Zola in the Vizetelly translations when he was a youth in the Potteries; and according to his autobiographical (and somewhat facetious) *The Truth About an Author*, one of his very early stories was modelled upon *L'Assommoir*: " It was a sinister narrative to illustrate the evils of marrying a drunken woman." If nowhere else, the story appears as the sub-plot of Daniel Povey and his wife in *The Old Wives' Tale*.

Realism, of course, is not the whole truth. " The notion that 'naturalists' have at last lighted on a final formula which insures truth to life," Bennett wrote in *The Author's Craft*, " is ridiculous. 'Naturalist' is merely an epithet expressing self-satisfaction." Nevertheless, Bennett observed the social scene carefully. In the manner of Zola preparing to write *Au Bonheur des Dames*, he studied the operation of the Savoy Hotel before he wrote *Imperial Palace*. Just as Zola went down into the mines to gather material for *Germinal*, so Bennett made expeditions into the industrial district of Clerkenwell to gather material for *Riceyman Steps*. He entitled the first chapter of *The Author's Craft* " Seeing Life."

It is Bennett the note-taker, Bennett the prosaic realist, whom Virginia Woolf depicts in her essay *Mr. Bennett and Mrs. Brown*. She sees him as an artist preoccupied with externals, incapable of penetrating beneath the surface of life to perceive character. (Bennett's portrayal of the strikers is superficial; it is men in the mass, seen and heard, undistinguished from each other.) Mrs. Woolf's criticism has had wide influence. One of the most recent writers on Bennett, James Hall, subscribes to it when he says that " Bennett, unwilling to see experience in these ways [psychological and anthropological], stops at a sociological and common-sense view of personality." As the prime document in the case against Bennett, Mrs. Woolf's essay requires appraisal.

Her essay is, more than anything else, a manifesto of the new art of the novel which sprang up with Lawrence, Forster, Joyce, and Woolf herself; and, in the manner of manifestoes, it cries down the old art of Bennett, Galsworthy, and Wells—mainly of Bennett, for he is considered by Mrs. Woolf to be the most important of the three. Mrs. Woolf's argument is as follows. Bennett and she are agreed that character is the foundation of fiction. Bennett, though, after all tribute has been paid to his skill in his craft, thinks that he has characterized successfully when he has clothed a name such as Hilda Lessways (the heroine of the *Clayhanger* trilogy), given the name some facial characteristics, put the name in a house, and put the house in a village. Bennett gives his readers some externals, some appurtenances, and imagines that he has characterized the person. And such is the force of convention that readers will believe that they know Hilda when they know this external information. The convention is no longer of much use to writers; the world has changed since 1910, and even human nature has changed; the new writers must devise methods and build conventions that will bring them closer to their characters. That they have not yet succeeded, one may admit; but they know the method that will not avail them anything: the method of Bennett.

The Mrs. Brown of Mrs. Woolf's title is a mythical woman riding in a railway carriage from Richmond to Waterloo. She is the person whom art must describe. She is the person, Mrs. Woolf asserts, whom Galsworthy describes by making her a victim of social injustice, whom Wells describes by creating a utopia for her (both men being more preoccupied with their visions of injustice and felicity than with Mrs. Bown), and whom Bennett describes by noticing the details of the carriage, Mrs. Brown's clothing, the cost of her brooch, its place of purchase, the social caste of the other riders, etc. Mrs. Woolf herself then undertakes to describe Mrs. Brown. She gives the woman's age, describes her clothing, notes a pinched face and small feet, gives some fragments of a conversation; she imagines the woman's house, full of her husband's model ships and medals, imagines a son gone to the bad; she believes the woman to be proud, heroic, tragic. Then Mrs. Woolf admits her own failure, that she has not got any closer to Mrs. Brown than Arnold Bennett has; and she blames him along with Galsworthy and Wells: " I have told you nothing whatever about her. But that is partly the great Edwardians' fault.

I asked them—they are my elders and betters. . . ." Her
essay comes only to the point that she and others are going
to try to get closer.

One can allow as the prerogative of youth the right to
destroy old gods, and one can acknowledge that if not in
her essay at least in her novels Mrs. Woolf approached Mrs.
Brown in ways that Bennett did not—even while one thinks
that the dailiness of Clarissa Dalloway's life owes an in-
eradicable debt to the dailiness of the lives of realistic
heroines, and that in a long view of twentieth-century
fiction the aims and techniques in achieving both dailinesses
may seem more similar than different. One can also see,
after thirty-nine years, that Mrs. Woolf did not understand what the old god Bennett was up to (she did not
really ask him) ; and see that Mrs. Dalloway is no more
real than Hilda Lessways.

It would be appropriate to respond to Mrs. Woolf with
an analysis of Hilda Lessways (whose psychological collapse
following her mother's death provides a problem) , but an
earlier heroine, Sophia Baines, serves better, partly because
she is the only character whose creation Bennett has discussed at any length and partly because she is a simpler
character, created at the threshold of his mature understanding. When Bennett first conceived *The Old Wives'
Tale* in 1903, after having seen a grotesque middle-aged
woman in a Paris restaurant, he wrote in his *Journal*:

> I immediately thought of a long 10 or 15 thousand word
> short story, " The History of Two Old Women." I gave this
> woman a sister fat as herself. . . . One should have lived
> ordinarily, married prosaically, and become a widow. The
> other should become a whore. . . . And they live together in
> old age, not too rich, a nuisance to themselves and to others.

A letter to Frank Harris of November 30, 1908, just after
the novel was published, comments upon this original con-

ception of Sophia. " My original intention was to make
her a magnificent courtesan. But I altered this, after due
thought. I conceive that what she did in fact become was
just as interesting and as good as anything else." Another
journal * entry of July 19, 1907, three months before he
began writing the novel, shows him still entertaining
thoughts of an end for Sophia different from that in the
novel and at least in part different from the original conception. The entry begins with a description of a French
peasant woman seen the previous evening.

> She was an old woman harnessed to a cart containing mer-
> chandise whose nature I could not distinguish. On either
> side of her was harnessed a dog about as big as a pointer.
> An old man stalked majestically behind, at a distance of
> several yards, carrying a very long staff and uttering at
> regular intervals a mournful cry concerning his wares. The
> old woman was, in the accepted phrase, " little more than a
> brute," and there was no doubt about it, no concealment
> of it. . . .

> I knew that Sophie [*sic*], the second heroine of *The Old
> Wives' Tale*, was going to live in France and be almost
> French, and I felt a tremendous naughty temptation to make
> the daughter of the most respectable Bursley draper sink in
> the world and end her days as the companion of dogs in
> front of a cart. Why not? What an outcry in the literary
> columns of the British press! What foamings at the mouth
> of outraged critics! And how it would somehow serve them
> right and do them good! However, I successfully fought and
> slew the temptation. Only authors know the dazzling tempta-
> tions of authorship.

The obvious inference about the nature of Bennett's

---

* Here and elsewhere references to uncollected portions of Bennett's
journal are distinguished from references to the published *Journal*.

second thoughts on these two alternative fates for Sophia is that Sophia is a Five Towns girl, molded by her environment to be commonsensical, prudent, inhibited; she may seem to rebel against her heritage, but in the most subtle ways and in the end she must be compelled by it. Paris merely gives her a more striking background than Bursley gives Constance to show her true colors. The convention here is realistic: environment determines character and fate. Insofar as Bennett is a realist in this limited sense—a fact which must be given due importance—the inference is legitimate. Several auctorial comments and other material in the novel (noted especially by L. G. Johnson and J. B. Simons) support it. They must be read without the ironical coloring that, as was suggested in the Introduction, sometimes modifies their meaning.

Although Sophia rashly delivers herself into Gerald's hands in London, "a prudent, mysterious instinct" gave her forethought to put by some money in case of emergency. In forcing her reluctant lover to marry her, "this fragile slip of the Baines stock, unconsciously drawing upon the accumulated strength of generations of honest living . . . , put a defeat upon him." In Paris, confronted with his financial irresponsibility, Sophia was "forced by some instinct to think about prices—she who at home had scorned the narrowness of life in the Square. In the Square she was understood to be quite without common sense, hopelessly imprudent; yet here, a spring of sagacity seemed to be welling up in her all the time. . . ." When later she steals from Gerald, "the act was characteristic of her enterprise and of her fundamental prudence. Still later "all the Baines in her clutched at" the small satisfaction that she and Gerald had no debts. In her illness, when she lives with two poor prostitutes, she reflects upon one of the destinies that Bennett saved her from: "Goodness! If

I had been in her place [that of Madame Foucault, the older prostitute] I shouldn't have been like that. I should have been rich. I should have saved like a miser." Her destiny includes something like miserliness. At the Pension Frensham, where she carries on the Baines business tradition, her "sole interest was in her profits." Years later when Constance writes to her, she is impressed with the letter's "natural expression of the Baines character" and feels that in responding "she too must show her Baines blood." Lastly, when she returns home she seems to Constance just the same as years before. Constance's thought is that "nothing could change a Baines"; and Bennett adds, "It was true that Constance's Sophia had not changed."

One would be forgiven for suspecting that Sophia's character is comprehended by the phrase "provincial shopkeeper's daughter." She is surrounded, too, by a mass of external detail. In the first pages of the novel Bennett places her in her setting. In the first sentence he identifies "those two girls, Constance and Sophia Baines," and then turns to say that they live on the fifty-third parallel of latitude, that north of them lies the river Trent and further north lie the rivers Dane and Dove, that they live in the county of Staffordshire, that their Five Towns are shaped variously like a horse, a donkey, etc. He gives some facts on the history and industry of the Five Towns; he names the business establishments of St. Luke's Square; he describes the physical appearance of the Baines house. He notes the isolation of the Five Towns from the rest of England and hence its ignorance and self-pride; he notes the grimy fierce struggle for survival and implies the grimness of the people; he observes manufacture and commerce and recognizes the social hierarchy built upon them. He then returns to Sophia and Constance briefly, describes their physical appearance and makes a few bald assertions about their characters.

The method is, by and large, the method that Mrs. Woolf attributes to the Edwardians. Oddly enough, the main words by which she defines Mrs. Brown's character, "tragic, heroic, yet with a dash of the flighty," are similar to those by which Bennett defines Sophia, "tragic masterpiece," "heroic," and "capricious." The fact suggests that the method possesses more merit than Mrs. Woolf grants it, since Mrs. Brown and Sophia seem distinct in their possession of these qualities. But the method does not encompass Bennett's art or define his understanding of Sophia. The action of the novel displays a rather more complexly conceived girl.

In the scenes dealing with her early womanhood, Sophia shows herself to be hysterical, willful, and passionate. Both she and Constance "laugh nervously, with a trace of hysteria" when Samuel Povey comes upon them unexpectedly at the outset of the novel. Sophia abandons herself to hysteria after she surreptitiously pulls Povey's tooth. When she quarrels with her mother over becoming a teacher, "her face was transfigured by uncontrollable passion; 'You all want to make me miserable!' she shrieked with terrible violence." Her willfulness displays itself in her devious enlistment of the support of Miss Chetwynd to force her mother to agree to the teaching career, then the abandoning of this career in a passionate moment after the death of her father. It shows itself in the secret rendezvous in the country that she arranges with Gerald. She goes to that rendezvous thinking, "I am a wicked girl"; presently she feels "as helpless as though she had been in a balloon with him"; then suddenly with a "transformed face . . . a haughty gesture" she rejects him: "She showed him her proud back and nodding head and wrathful skirts; and hurried off without a word, almost running." When she and Gerald are in London, she displays herself similarly; prior to her

wrath and tears when she realizes that he does not intend
to marry her, she greets him very ardently: " her ardour
was exceeding his . . . , the powerful clinging of her lips
somewhat startled his senses. . . ."

The Sophia of four years later is a modified woman; the
fires of hysteria, willfulness, and passion are being banked;
a restrained and cold woman is emerging. When Gerald
tells her he has no money left, the occasion is not one for
hysteria. Sophia merely replies, " Well, and what do you
expect *me* to do? " Bennett adds:

> The accent, at once ironic and listless, in which she put
> this question, showed that strange and vital things had hap-
> pened to Sophia. . . . It did really seem to her, indeed, that
> the Sophia whom Gerald had espoused was dead and gone,
> and that another Sophia had come into her body. . . . And
> though this was but a seeming, though she was still the same
> Sophia more fully disclosed, it was a true seeming. . . .
> She was ready to pay the price of pride and of a moment's
> imbecility with a lifetime of self-repression.

The metamorphosis is by no means complete. When Gerald
deserts Sophia the next day, she becomes ill and undergoes
the delirium of several days in which she sees herself dying.
From the sickbed arises the woman who when old Niepce
entreats her to remain calm about his indecent proposal
" showed no sign of not remaining calm." When later the
same night Chirac accuses her of selling herself to Niepce,
" she felt that she too ought to be theatrical. . . . But she
was not capable. . . ." Afterward she cries, but not hysterically: " She wept gently for a very long time." When Chirac
proposes to her a few days later she rejects him with no
internal storm of feeling, only a vague curiosity as to why
she does so. The explanation that Bennett gives for her
refusal, that " her desires had . . . been laid to sleep by
excessive physical industry and nervous strain," points to

the conscious way in which she is remolding herself: through absorption in the physical and financial tasks of maintaining her boarding house. The siege of Paris provides a good occasion for her industry, but she probably does not need it; she preoccupies herself as successfully when peace comes. The only subsequent outcropping of the uncontrollable self is the twitching of the mouth that develops when Matthew Peel-Swinnerton recognizes her years later.

The first point to make about this characterization is that at the outset Sophia shows herself to be a very different person from her Five Towns sister. Environment has not been able to make them the same. Constance can show a trace of hysteria along with Sophia when Samuel Povey comes on them, but there is a basic psychological difference between the two girls that is suggested in the first scene in the novel when they watch the servant Maggie go up the street to a rendezvous with a lover: " It's too ridiculous! " says Sophia; " Poor old Maggie! " says Constance. Secondly, the character development that Sophia undergoes cannot be explained in ordinary environmental terms. Some sort of psychological theory must be invoked. The most ready explanation is that Sophia's character develops in response to a series of shocks. These shocks arise from events in the external world that Sophia experiences, but they cannot be said to be deterministic in the ordinary sense of environmental determinism.

Specifically, Sophia's response to shock is self-repression. The shock of her father's death, all the more dreadful because she is in part to blame for it, brings a renunciation of her dream of becoming a teacher: " In the splendour of her remorse for a fatal forgetfulness, she had renounced that which she loved and thrown herself into that which she loathed." Later she undergoes the shock of seeing the execution of Rivain. She does not want to go to the execution; she refuses to participate in the revelry; " 'I cannot stand this! ' she told herself in horror, but she could not move; she could not move even her eyes." Four years afterward she undergoes the shock of Gerald's desertion. She has learned in other moments of shock in their relationship that she has taken up with a rogue; yet she has remained with him: she has been " ready to pay the price of pride and of a moment's imbecility with a lifetime of self-repression." The shock on this occasion produces a retreat from the world, her illness, during which she is " perfectly aware that she was going to die." From her illness emerges gradually the new woman, stern, cold, morally incorruptible. Her actual death in the novel follows upon another shock, " the most violent shock that she had ever had." Thirty-six years after Gerald's desertion, she goes to see him in Manchester, where he supposedly lies ill. He is dead. The shock of seeing him and remembering him as he once was, strong and young, and of seeing herself in the mirror, an old forlorn woman whom he and others had once desired, kills her. She does not blame him for her history, but his dead body evokes it. " ' My life has been too terrible! ' she thought. ' I wish I was dead. I have been through too much. It is monstrous, and I cannot stand it. I do not want to die, but I wish I was dead.' " She dies that night.

Such an explanation of Sophia's development is helpful, but it is no more adequate than the theory of environmental determinism. One can go deeper with Bennett's blessing. He wrote to a woman friend about *The Old Wives' Tale*—presumably exaggerating for her benefit—" I will admit . . . that no English novelist ever suggested more unspeakable things, and got away without being understood, than me in that book." The unspeakable things point toward a psychological element that has less of the accidental and external to it. Two actions of Sophia's youth suggest psychological determinism. The first is her pulling of Samuel Povey's tooth at the outset of the novel. Her boldness here distinguishes her from Constance; psychologically her act suggests a cold, hard feminine quality rather than a warm, generous one. The second action concerns Sophia's first sexual adventure, her flirting with Gerald Scales. She deserts her bedridden father upon seeing Gerald approaching the shop; she runs down into the shop and grabs a pair of scissors and then starts to hurry off, " as though the scissors had been a grail, passionately sought and to be jealously hidden away." She is called to, and when Gerald comes up to her and while she stands flirting with him, she is " playing nervously with the scissors." The defensive and aggressive implications of Sophia's holding the scissors are confirmed by her later actions with Gerald: her rejection of his sexual playfulness when they go for a walk together, her rejection of him in London, etc. Comparable implications surround another occasion when Sophia wants a pair of scissors: years later when she lies ill in Paris and thinks she is going to die, she deliriously " cried aloud for a pair of scissors. She wanted to cut off her hair . . . , she fought for the scissors." Upon waking from the delirium she learns that she has assaulted Madame Foucault.

The sexual hostility suggested in the tooth-pulling and the playing with the scissors becomes clearer in later action. When Sophia and Gerald go to observe the guillotining of Rivain, Gerald parades about with a prostitute; but as soon as Rivain is executed, Gerald collapses: " the very image of death . . . flaccid . . . shamed. . . ." Sophia regards him with the utmost sexual scorn: " He did not possess even enough spirit to play the *rôle* of roysterer to the end . . . ; she could have thrashed him. . . ." Most obvious, perhaps, is the scene in which Sophia ends her marriage with Gerald.

She has watched him go out, purchase a cigar, and go off with a prostitute. When he returns, she is contemptuous toward him, and she ends their relationship by showing him the red circlet of paper from the cigar. Out of context, the implication is all too obvious; it presumably includes not only Gerald's illicit intercourse with the prostitute but also Sophia's utter refusal of him. Sophia thinks: " He had made her suffer, but she was almost repaid for everything by that moment of cruel triumph [of showing him the empty ring]." Subsequently in her life Sophia attracts and then rejects other men, notably Niepce and Chirac. At the end of the novel, when Gerald is dead in Manchester, Sophia stands over his body and thinks of her lost youth: " Could she excite lust now? Ah! the irony of such a question! " The irony is in part that she excited lust in order to destroy it.

The tooth-pulling, the playing with the scissors, the displaying of the cigar ring, and Sophia's general rejection of men suggest a consistency of character underlying the undoubted changes through which Sophia passes. This consistency gives weight to Bennett's words in the scene in which Gerald tells Sophia he has no money left (that " she was still the same Sophia more fully disclosed ") and to his remark upon the reunion of the sisters (that " Constance's Sophia had not changed "). At the same time it seems to preclude the exercise of free will implied in the comment that Sophia need not have rejected Chirac: " Perhaps if her desires had not been laid to sleep by excessive physical industry and nervous strain, the sequel might have been different." The occasions on which a person of rigid character displays himself are offered by chances, hazards of human life; these chances afford opportunities for the person simply to show what he is. The case appears to be different with Sophia. In contrast to almost all of his novels after *Clayhanger*, Bennett deals here with a great span of years, in which Sophia along with other characters is given an opportunity not merely to prove herself in the ordinary sense of the word but also to prove herself in the sense of testing herself. Sophia's character has not been rigidly determined by her environment, by psychological shocks in her youth and maturity, or by some hypothetical psychological twist during childhood. These things are determinants, or may be, but in her very experience of them she is the agent who must make choices of responses. Her past experiences and actions do not irrevocably control her future experiences and actions but rather interact with them in a motion that is self-determining. The limits to this motion are set only by a certain given quality that is the core of the person who is Sophia.

The evidence that Bennett takes this view is suggested in the crucial passage in which he remarks that Sophia might well have accepted Chirac's offer, and in an earlier passage when Sophia accepts the proposal of Madame Foucault to share her business: " Sophia had a purpose in existence; she had a fluid soul to mould to her will according to her wisdom. . . ." The evidence lies also in some parallels between Sophia and three prostitutes in the novel. When Sophia and Gerald are in Paris for the first time, he tells her of the impending execution of Rivain, who has killed Claudine Jacquinot, " a tremendous—er—wrong 'un here in the forties. Made a lot of money, and retired to her native town." Claudine's situation is somewhat like Sophia's. Sophia has shamed herself in the eyes of her mother by eloping with Gerald and has stolen money from her aunt in doing so. After Gerald deserts her she lives with two prostitutes for a time and is asked by each of them to join them in their activities. Reflecting upon the poverty of one of them she says to herself, " Goodness! If I had been in her place, I shouldn't have been like that. I should have been rich." She joins the same one in conducting the boarding house and later when she runs it alone is offered money for her favors by Niepce. Later she owns the Pension Frensham, furnished in part from the prostitute's house. She becomes rich. She returns to her native town.

That Bennett when he first planned the novel intended that Sophia should become a prostitute, and that in rejecting this end he nevertheless involved her intimately with two prostitutes and made her life recapitulate the life of another prostitute, suggest that the girl he had in mind when he sat down to write the novel could very well have become a prostitute. That she does not become one lies with her creator rather than with Bursley society or psychological experience. Not that she could have become another Madame Foucault. Sophia herself is clear on the point: " I shouldn't have been like that." She would have become a respectable prostitute, calculating, cold, efficient, moral. Sophia might have done anything; the limitation would have been in the manner of her doing. " The foundation of her character," Bennett says at the same point at which he suggests that she might have become Chirac's mistress, " was a haughty moral independence." This is the core of the person Sophia. It is the absolute determinant of her actions; it is autonomous.

One sees Sophia in a new light. Why is it that her response to " What Life Is " (the title of Book Four of the novel) is so different from that of Constance? Constance at the end, when she is sick and on the verge of being driven from the family home, when she has lost her son to London and seen Sophia die, thinks of her life " with a sort of tart but not sour cheerfulness: ' *Well, that is what life is!* ' Sophia at the end, when she confronts the dead Gerald, thinks of her life, " It is monstrous." In the course of the novel Constance undergoes shocks as grave as those that affect Sophia: childbirth, the slow death of Samuel, Cyril's abandoning her. Life is never monstrous for her. It is monstrous for the girl and woman of haughty moral independence; it is an invasion of her self, a wound in her soul. From the very beginning she was armed against life; she feels its wound all the more deeply.

Mrs. Woolf concluded her essay on Bennett by averring that " we are trembling on the verge of one of the great ages of English literature. But it can only be reached if we are determined never, never to desert Mrs. Brown." She thought Bennett had deserted Mrs. Brown to describe the railway carriage. Many years afterward Philip Rahv wrote an essay called " Mrs. Woolf and Mrs. Brown," in which he asserted that Mrs. Woolf herself ended by deserting reality; he felt that Bennett's Mrs. Brown, née Sophia Baines, was more substantial. Be this as it may, Mrs. Woolf spent some time looking for Mrs. Brown. To her preoccupation one may ascribe her failure to look at Mr. Bennett.

CHAPTER 2

Psychological Realism

RICEYMAN STEPS
LORD RAINGO

FOR ALL HER reality, for all the sophistication of Bennett's conception of her, Sophia Baines is an ordinary person. A rounded, complex figure she may be, but she lacks depths, lacks profundity. Bennett drew her, presumably, from some rounded, complex, but still ordinary women that he had known in the provinces and in the city. Sophia is like most heroines in fiction. She is like Clarissa Harlowe (that other heroine who rejects all men), whose life is devoted too much to discriminations of feelings, to proprieties of behavior. She is like Clarissa Dalloway, whose life is devoted too much to nuances of sensation and social conduct—as Virginia Woolf undoubtedly thought in modelling her after Lady Ottoline Morell. She is like these heroines in that her special interest for us is literary; if we met her in the provinces or in the city, we would recognize a familiar, ordinary face.

There are some characters in fiction who strike us differently: Raskolnikov, Lord Jim. They may be—more often than not, they are—relatively simple characters, observed not in the round but observed flatly; yet they have depths, or they seem to have depths because they shake us to our depths. The difference is easy to exaggerate and yet impossible to exaggerate. Lord Jim is in many ways an ordinary person; Conrad says that at most he is "not a type of wide commonness." Yet to Marlow, Jim is "in the forefront of his kind, as if the obscure truth involved were momentous enough to affect mankind's conception of itself." One might also say that Jim is Everyman and hence no man, that his struggle is a symbolic action, an objectification of the struggle within man between the irrational and the moral self, that Conrad is arguing the necessity of establishing a new balance between the two forces. Whatever else one says, Jim seems to have a more profound soul—or reveals himself more profoundly—than most other fictional persons.

Bennett is not Conrad, let alone Dostoevsky. His customary wry detachment from his characters militates against the reader's identifying himself intimately with them and so sensing their depths. He has not Conrad's compulsion to write in the first person. Nevertheless, there are two novels in the Bennett canon whose heroes occasionally reveal Conradian or Dostoevskian depths. Both novels are late works, supposedly products of an artist of declining powers. One of them, *Riceyman Steps,* is usually seen as a clinical study of a miser; the other, *Lord Raingo,* is commonly regarded as a political *roman à clef.* They are narrowly conceived books, just as *Lord Jim* is; they lack the scope of *The Old Wives' Tale;* they are—according to the sort of judgment that places a great epic ahead of a great dramatic lyric—smaller works than *The Old Wives' Tale.* But in what they achieve, the disclosure of the passionate depths of two men, they are Bennett's best novels.

Riceyman Steps relates the last year in the life of a miser, Henry Earlforward. It describes his courtship of a miserly woman, his marriage, and his self-destruction. The novel is, in a superficial sense, Balzacian rather than Conradian or Dostoevskian. Earlforward in his passion resembles

Balzac's miserly Grandet, and the servant Elsie can be compared in character and action to Eugénie. The novel is also a novel of the grotesque, Bennett's only serious work that can be so described. By and large, Bennett avoids or minimizes grotesqueness, especially in character. He wrote once to Wells, " The strongly marked character, the eccentric, the sharply defined type, is the easiest thing in the world to do (you wouldn't believe how I despise my Meshach Myatt [a character in *Leonora*] as a creation)." If anything, though, Bennett's novel is more grotesque than Balzac's; for Bennett isolates Earlforward much more from society and from contemporary events than Balzac isolates Grandet, Bennett gives more consistent attention to Earlforward than Balzac gives to Grandet, and Bennett requires his subsidiary figures to share Earlforward's qualities more than Balzac requires his to share Grandet's. Nevertheless, Earlforward's grotesqueness is his significant feature only from a certain perspective; from another, his significant feature is that which he shares with everyone: a profound preoccupation with love and death.

Earlforward keeps a secondhand bookshop. He is not particularly eager either to buy or to sell books; and if he buys a valuable book for little money, he will sell it for little money. He is not so much interested in acquiring money as in hoarding what he has; and when he has to part with any of his wealth, he sooner parts with a book worth two pounds than with a ten-shilling note. Money alone—not even checks—is his passion, and he cares most for hard money. In more than forty years he has had no other passion. Then into his life—at the outset of the novel —comes Violet Arb. It is in the contest between his two passions that the novel works itself out.

On the surface Earlforward appears " quiet, intelligent, refined, and kindly." He has " full red lips and . . . [a]

fresh complexion." So Violet Arb and others see him at the beginning. Violet recognizes that he has "reserves, both of character and of goods," but considers him "nearly fault-less." Not until she inspects his shop one day in his absence does she obtain some hint of the man behind the mask. The shop is an image of Earlforward: "The first bay was well-lighted and tidy; but the others, as they receded into the gloomy backward of the shop, were darker and darker, untidier and untidier. The effect was of mysterious and vast populations of books imprisoned for ever in everlasting shade, chained, deprived of air and sun and movement, hopeless, resigned, martyrised." (The latter portion of this description parallels two descriptions of Earlforward at the end of the book, when Dr. Raste visits him for the last time and when Mr. Belrose discovers him dead.) Violet is fright-ened by what the shop intimates about its master; but she thinks romantically—being foolish as well as deeply maso-chistic: "Could . . . [I] not tame monsters?" Later, when they are married, she sees the heart of his shop, the safe in which he keeps his gold; and still later she learns that the safe is his heart: "But what I say is," she cries at him in a rage because of his sexual coldness, "I'd sooner be knocked about a bit and know what my man's really think-ing about than live with a locked-up cast-iron safe like you."

Earlforward's struggle in the novel is to protect his cast-iron safe, to protect his passion, to preserve his integrity, to hold inviolate his inmost self. His enemy is his own sexual desire; but as he views the problem, his enemy is the object of his passion, Violet, and through her the servant Elsie. (Note the suggestion of both passion and violation in Violet's name.) His sexual desires have lain dormant for many years, undisturbed by Elsie's obvious physical charms or her masochism. What Earlforward wants of Elsie is only that "she should grow old for him in sterile celibacy." His desires are instead aroused by a woman at menopause who possesses a more subtle kind of masochism. He thinks of her as "girlish" and "masterful," and he likes her because she is a miser too; but fundamentally he is attracted to her sterility and her self-destructive urge. His sexual desire cannot countenance life; it does not exist where there is life; it is not life-giving but life-denying. What he fails to understand about his sexual desire as it first inflames him is that it will require him to give something of himself (who has never willingly given anything to anyone) and that it will result in an invasion of his physical and spiritual privacy (which have hitherto been impregnable). He does not realize that his two passions must war against each other. He does not see that his sterile self-love (for which his miserliness is the symbol) must conflict with his life-denying sexual love (for which his limp is the symbol). He thinks of his sexual role only: "there's *that*! Want some getting used to!"

In the first stage of their relationship, Violet achieves some triumphs over Earlforward's private passion, and Earlforward seems to accept the triumphs with good grace. She refuses to pay more than sixpence for a cookbook that he offers to sell her for a shilling, and in admiration for her miserliness he gives the book to her. On another occasion she manages to avoid paying a bet that she has made with him, and "he admired her the more for her genial feminine unscrupulousness." It is on their wedding day that she achieves her most serious triumphs over him: she forces him to spend money, and she invades his privacy. At Madame Tussaud's, where they go on their wedding trip, she wants Earlforward to pay eightpence extra to go into the Chamber of Horrors—not clearly realizing yet that she has an untamed monster by her side. Earlforward recognizes the monster: "He turned pale; he could not speak;

he was himself amazed at the power of his passion [of miserliness]. Full of fine intentions, he dared not affront the monster. Then, his throat dry and constricted, he said blandly, with an invisible gesture of the most magnificent and extravagant heroism: ' I hardly think we ought to consider expense on a day like this.' And the monster recoiled, and Henry [Earlforward] wiped his brow." They return home from Madame Tussaud's, and Earlforward finds that as her wedding present to him Violet has had the shop professionally vacuum-cleaned. The significance of the act does not escape him. The cleaning is not a gift but a robbery, an invasion, of a miser's house and soul: " He had been robbed of something. And the place had lost its look of home; it was bare, inhospitable, and he was a stranger in it." He is robbed of dirt, dirt in which nothing grows into life; he asks the men about the dirt: " Do you sell it? Do you get anything for it?" He tells Violet that he is not vexed; he acknowledges to himself the "grandeur" of her act.

The incident that outwardly symbolizes Violet's triumph, the triumph of sexual love over Earlforward's private passion, is their eating of the wedding cake that Elsie gives them. They both lose restraint; they abandon themselves to their sensual appetite. " They could afford to be young and to live perilously, madly, absurdly. They lost control of themselves, and gloried in so doing." More especially Earlforward: " ' I am living! ' shouted an unheard voice in Henry's soul."

The triumph is outward, partial, pyrrhic. The woman who invades Earlforward's house and soul is trapped therein. House and soul are made of cast-iron. In a while Violet will realize fully " that she had passed under the domination of her bland Henry. It was as if she had entered a fortress and heard the self-locking gates thereof clang behind her. No escape! " The very symbol of her triumph is the sign of her defeat; the devouring of the wedding cake points to the strategy by which Earlforward will destroy her. For in that grotesque moment in which he feels most alive, he develops the indigestion that is the first cause of his starving himself, of his starving Violet sexually, of his cancer. The cake that he devours so ravenously seems "a danger to existence. . . . It seemed unconquerable. It seemed more fatal than daggers or gelignite." It is. At the end of the novel Elsie punishes herself for Earlforward's death: " She had noticed that he had never been the same since the orgy of her wedding-cake, and she had a terrible suspicion that immoderate wedding-cake caused cancer [Earlforward's cancer is located at the juncture of the gullet and the cardiac end of the stomach]. Thus she added one more to the uncounted theories of the origin of cancer, and nobody yet knows enough of the subject to be able to disprove Elsie's theory." The resolution of Earlforward's conflict is automatic. To yield to sexual passion, to open his cast-iron safe to another person, is to invite robbery, corruption; by these he dies; but to die is to cut off sexual passion, to close his cast-iron safe.

The nature of Earlforward's strategy is first suggested when he takes Violet for a walk one Sunday before he has proposed to her. She intends to leave the district, and Earlforward sees his sexual passion thwarted. His bad knee, the cause of his limp, begins to ache. He thinks that " his body and his mind were always reacting upon one another. ' Why should my knee ache because I'm bothered? ' he thought, and could give no answer. But in secret he was rather proud of these mysterious inconvenient reactions." He continues walking, despite the fact that the ache soon becomes torture to him: " he perceived, dimly through the veil of his physical pain, that their intimacy was developing on the right lines." In an image prefiguring his cancer, he feels "death in his very stomach." He also continues walking because he will not pay money for a taxicab to take them home. " His fear now was lest his grand passion [miserliness] should on this occasion be overcome by bodily weakness. He did not desire it to be overcome. He desired it to conquer even if it should kill him." His limp, a symbol of his sexual inadequacy, is also a symbol of the conventional weakness of the flesh, his sexual desire. Physical pain and sexual love become virtually synonymous; Earlforward will defeat them by enduring them until they kill him; his very enduring of them will preserve his spiritual passion. His strategy might seem strange, but it is not strange to him. It is as clear to his conscious and unconscious minds as is the strategy of a Christian saint, who preserves the spirit by mortifying the flesh. Not accidentally Earlforward perceives his strategy on a Sunday morning. He and Violet walk over to St. John's Square and there inspect the tablet on the Priory Church of the Order of St. John of Jerusalem (another name for John the Baptist, who was made a martyr by a woman whose attractions he scorned).

The course of Earlforward's strategy runs true. Shortly after his marriage he begins to starve himself and Violet. He denies himself food and he denies her his body. Violet understands. The sterile woman tries to make him eat an egg one morning. He refuses. She cries out, " And what's the use of a husband who doesn't eat enough I should like to know! " Earlforward blushes. In the evening she cooks a steak especially for him. He says he has indigestion. She works herself into a rage. She says his indigestion is only an excuse for his miserliness. He won't spend money. He's stingy, stingy in all ways: " Love? a lot you know about it! Cold by day and cold by night! " Earlforward is not disturbed. He simply sees consciously for the first time that " he must count her in the future as the enemy of his passion [miserliness] and plot accordingly." His plot is to retreat to his bed, and his explanation is that he must punish Elsie for stealing food. (Elsie eats the precious egg that he refuses; she devours the steak that he will not touch. Elsie is well fed but hungry: her lover is away.)

Earlforward's indigestion, of course, stems from his cancer. And his loss of sexual appetite naturally follows from his starvation. But his cancer is metaphorical and psychological as well as actual. The grotesquerie of his plot against Elsie makes the point clear. On the night before, at Elsie's instigation, Dr. Raste had come to see Earlforward; but Earlforward had protested his good health, and Raste had instead examined Violet. Now, still refusing to admit to Violet that he is ill, he calls Elsie into the bedroom and says to her, " I'm very ill, Elsie, and I shall probably never get up again. Do you think it's right of you to go on stealing food as you do with a dying man in the house? " Later in the evening he becomes violently ill, yet refuses to go to the hospital as Raste recommends, and finally acquiesces only after Violet becomes hysterical; but when morning comes and he is to be taken off, he is again adamant and seems to Elsie " a martyr to anguish and pain, a tiger hunted and turning ferociously on his pursuers." In Raste's final effort to get Earlforward to the hospital he says to the miser, " It's no use me telling you how ill you are because you know as well as I do how ill you are." Earlforward quietly replies, " I don't think I'll go into a hospital, doctor." Raste, beaten, turns to Elsie and says that if Earlforward dies, he, the doctor, will refuse to give a certificate of the cause of death. Raste says these words " with implacable and calculated cruelty." They do not disturb Earlforward:

Mr. Earlforward only laughed, a short, dry sardonic laugh.
The sun shone into the silent room and upon the tumbled

bed and the sick triumphant man, and made them more
terrible than midnight could have made them.

In the brief image—one of Bennett's finest artistic strokes—
the culminating image in the characterization of Earlforward, the soul of the man lies bare.

The rest of the novel is dénouement. Violet dies before
Earlforward does; she dies from undernourishment following an operation for a benign tumor. Since both the undernourishment and the tumor can be indirectly attributed to
Earlforward (the tumor, according to Dr. Raste, stems
from her childlessness), he may be said to have disposed
of the enemy of his passion. He very definitely manages to
remove her from his house in the ludicrous mix-up over his
and her going to the hospital. And as a token of his victory,
he gets up from his bed after he hears of her death. But
he has too nearly destroyed himself in his struggle, and he
fails to reckon with another enemy of his passion, Elsie.
He totters from his bedroom into his den, where his safe
lies; he intends with "superhuman courage to recreate his
existence over the ruins of it"; he sits down to do some
work. Then he discovers for the second time that he has
been robbed: he opens his safe and discovers that Elsie has
taken sixpence out of it (to pay for a messenger to go to
Violet in the hospital). His house, his safe, and his soul
have been invaded. "Life was bigger, more cruel, more
awful than he had imagined." He can only die.

It is apparent from the incidental discussion of the subsidiary characters, Violet and Elsie, that Bennett has developed a complex study of love and death. Violet's character
can be explored in terms similar to Earlforward's, and Elsie's
romance with her soldier has something of the same character
as the relationship between Violet and Earlforward. In
giving such serious attention to his other characters, Bennett

detracts from the force with which Earlforward might otherwise hold us. Furthermore, Earlforward's grotesqueness,
along with the characteristic detachment with which he is
viewed, prevents an identification with him that would
strengthen the sense of his depths. It might be inferred
from these circumstances that Bennett's understanding of
Earlforward is clinical or abstract: he has read *Beyond the
Pleasure Principle.* It is true that he possessed some knowledge of Freudian views; and he was a close friend of W. H.
R. Rivers, the psychologist, who was sympathetic to the
Freudian outlook. But like other artists before him, he
understood human mentality without reading textbooks.
He was dealing with love and death with unusual penetration in 1909, in his novel *The Glimpse,* long before he
had read Freud or met Rivers.

Rivers remarked of Bennett that he possessed great em-
pathic capacity. And Bennett in *The Author's Craft,* referring to every writer but presumably thinking of himself
in particular, writes that "in his own individuality there
is something of everybody." Some facts from his life suggest
a close relationship to Earlforward. In his early London
years, he dealt in secondhand books, issuing around 1892
a couple of catalogues; and he remained throughout his
life an inveterate frequenter of secondhand bookshops and
for many years bought a book a day. He was in money
matters extremely meticulous (despite great generosity) ;
during most of his life he kept account of his minutest
daily expenditures. Thirdly, there is reason to believe that
he was a relatively cold man sexually (although he was in
other respects a man of great warmth). The detachment
that Bennett maintains in the novel is esthetic, principled;
it reflects his commitment to the realist tradition. In the
same year that he wrote *Riceyman Steps,* he wrote a preface
to his play *Don Juan* in which he makes clear the sympathy
with which he regards someone like Earlforward:

Whether the majority of readers or spectators will accept
my hero as sympathetic I doubt. They will probably say
that a true gentleman who in pursuit of an ideal humiliates
the pride of his brother by public flagellation and drives
women to murder and suicide, cannot by any standard be
sympathetic. But for me the point is that my Don Juan
has an ideal. He is not a sensualist; he is an idealist. He
is passionately hungering for perfection. . . .

In *Lord Raingo,* written three years after *Riceyman Steps,*
Bennett discloses the soul of another man preoccupied with
love and death. As a comparison of the titles suggests,
Bennett is less concerned in the later novel with a physical
scene with which to symbolize his hero's mind; he focuses
his attention more consistently upon the man himself. He
also makes Raingo much more the main figure of the novel
than Earlforward is of *Riceyman Steps.* And he makes him
a normal person, with whom the reader is more likely to
identify himself. The consequence is that *Lord Raingo* is
Bennett's most moving novel.

Against a background of a world at war, Samuel Raingo
lives out the last year of his life. The scene is the civilian
one, and Raingo's own war activities are confined to the
conduct of the Ministry of Records. The conflict impinges
upon him personally, however, with the return of his son
from a prisoner-of-war camp and with the suicide of his
mistress following upon the death of a soldier to whom
she was attached. Raingo in 1918 is fifty-five years old and
has a heart condition that might mean death in five or ten
years—although the doctor who examines him in the opening chapter dismisses the prognosis of other doctors, warning
him only to be careful to avoid pneumonia. He feels, withal,
young in heart: he is " as a boy " when the doctor reassures
him of his health; he is " vitalized, young," " absurdly . . .
so," on occasions when he goes to his mistress; he is " a

youth " when he goes to encounter the prime minister, and feels " like a schoolboy " upon the successful conclusion of his encounter. Throughout Part One the image recurs: when he first examines a secret document, when upon the illness of the prime minister's mother he reaffirms his duty in his war work, when he is raised to the peerage, and when he triumphs over his enemies. Death he cannot escape, though; " death was in his heart "; death he pursues.

Raingo takes a risk with his heart. In the past few years he had been " near death from inanition," the result of protecting his heart; he now courts death from life, the war work he takes on. The irony is multifold. In his first interview with the prime minister, he employs his weak heart strategically. First, in order that he will not be in everlasting indebtedness to the prime minister for obtaining the ministry for him, he pretends that his weak heart will not allow him to accept the portfolio. Second, in order that he might obtain a peerage, he says that he has been particularly warned against public speaking—which would be involved were he to take the proffered route to the ministry of standing for Commons. Raingo consciously exaggerates the danger; nevertheless, it is following a speech in the House of Lords—probably forced on him in part by the prime minister—that Raingo catches the pneumonia that leads to his death. Again there are ironies. His heart itself survives the strain of the speech and also of his few words at the press banquet that evening; his lungs, rather, are damaged by the speech; his whole system succumbs—enervated by his work, the machinations against him, and his culminating triumphant effort to redeem his position.

Still it is his heart that kills him. For he takes another risk with it. He falls in love. In a physical sense, he endangers his heart by sexual activity—and Delphine, his mistress, is solicitous (possibly for her own reasons) that

he not overexert himself with her and also that he see his
doctor regularly. The greater risk, though, is spiritual;
and it is in this respect that he feels "death . . . in his
heart." The knowledge that he is too old for Delphine,
that there is a younger man in her life ("Youth wanted
youth, and he was middle-aged," "I am mad! I am mad!")
tears his heart. From the very beginning, before he sees
Delphine with the soldier, he is consumed with jealous
fear, and every visit to her apartment causes anguish. Initially he finds no ground for his suspicions: the supposed
young man hiding in the next room turns out to be Gwen,
Delphine's half-sister. (Gwen's hysterical words at the end
of the book suggest that the personal relationship between
the two women may be homosexual.) Upon his second
visit he finds Delphine gone and later observes her with
the soldier at the Savoy. On the third visit, thinking the
soldier might be there, he feels that "jealousy . . . furious
and gigantic . . . killed everything else in his mind." Yet
the same visit, like others, "was the summit of life for
him." Ultimately, just at the point of his political triumph,
Delphine deserts him, and he believes she has gone off with
her soldier. Disabused of this notion by Gwen, he thinks
that "I was too old for her, and she was too kind to tell
me so." Then he discovers that Delphine (who is portrayed
as a melancholic) has committed suicide, and learns also
that her soldier has recently been killed in action; and
he thinks again that her suicide is an act of love for the
soldier. Gwen insists, though, that Delphine had maintained
the relationship with the soldier out of compassion (she
had once been engaged to him) and had in fact quarrelled
violently with him before he had returned to the front.
She thinks that Delphine has committed suicide for two
reasons: in self-punishment over the soldier ("she must
have thought she'd killed him—I mean made him want to

be killed ") and in self-abnegation with regard to Raingo
(" she said to me once that you ought to get married
[Raingo's wife, Adela, has died], but she couldn't face being
Lady Raingo, and you'd never marry anyone else as long
as she was alive ").

Raingo, then, bears responsibility for Delphine's death.
He thinks that Gwen " had practically accused him . . . of
causing the death of her beloved, self-sacrificing sister! "
He also has some guilt with regard to his wife's death.
Ostensibly Adela's death is due to her having accidentally
run her automobile into a ditch and turned it over. She
is a bad driver. Raingo's exclamation when he reads the
telegram saying only that she has been in a serious accident
—" I always knew that woman would kill herself one of
these days "—can be regarded as a manner of speaking
rather than as an acknowledgment that his infidelity has
given her reason for despair. Nevertheless, Raingo's employee Wrenkin remarks, " She must have been going at
a rare pace. I know that car. It wouldn't turn over at any
ordinary speed, and the ditch isn't deep." Raingo later
goes through the drawers of her desk, " spying upon her,"
as though looking for some evidence that knowledge of his
liaison might have driven her to suicide.

More important, perhaps, is Raingo's confusion of Adela
with Delphine, with the consequence that whatever guilt
he feels toward one he feels towards the other. At one
point Bennett says, " No two women could have been more
different from one another than Adela and Delphine. But
for Sam in that moment they were alike." On several
occasions Raingo's acts or feelings towards the two women
suggest their single psychological identity for him. He is
perturbed when on the day of his elevation to the peerage
both of them greet him with, " Well, my lord "; he asks
Wrenkin whether Adela's face has been disfigured by her

death and asks Gwen the same of Delphine; and in the
last moment of his delirium before death he imagines himself with Delphine, but the name he murmurs is "Adela."
It is relevant too that the two women's names are similar,
and suggest sisterhood.

The death in Raingo's heart is his will to die, first in his
overburdening his heart with work and with love, and
secondly in his remorse for the deaths of Delphine and
Adela. He does not die of pneumonia; in a week he is
recovering, receiving visits from political friends and receiving a gift from the prime minister's mother—a miniature
Virgin—that immensely comforts him. Then Gwen accuses
him along with the soldier of having killed Delphine: "You
and Harry Point have killed my poor adored sister between
you." He tries to reject the notion as absurd and agonizes
himself again with the thought that Delphine died for love
of the soldier. "He was on the way to recovery, and he
did not care." On the next morning the elation that had
pervaded the sick-room has disappeared; pleurisy has supervened and pericarditis threatens. The operation for pleurisy
is momentarily successful; but Raingo does not care. The
succeeding blows to his system are psychological and spiritual: the miniature Virgin falling to the floor, the failure
of Mrs. Blacklow (to whom Raingo ascribes uncanny powers)
to prophesy his recovery, Geoffrey's assumption of power
of attorney, the nurse's praying for him, and lastly Gwen's
hysterical reiteration of her charge.

At an earlier point in the novel, Raingo contemplates
the pregnant Mrs. Blacklow and thinks to himself, "The
meaning of war was within her." Raingo does not explore
the thought; he is not a thoughtful man, and the novel is
not a philosophical novel. He understands it in the depths
of his soul. Later he contemplates Mrs. Blacklow again
and has a "vision of Delphine carrying *his* happy child

in her glorious body "; but now Delphine is dead and he is dying, and the thought of her pregnancy " electrified and desolated him. Dead! Dead! " He asks himself why Delphine committed suicide and answers himself:

> She had in her the fatal seed of death. She was appointed to unhappiness for herself, and to spread unhappiness round her like a contagion. Yet with her he had been at moments marvelously happy—too happy to recall his irrecoverable bliss without the direst pain. Yes, they had been united— she, in her magnificent beauty, and he—he the wasted, unshaven, broken, wrecked, panting, poor old thing on the bed. Yes, she had loved him. Yes, her honest arms had folded him in love. But all the time the seed of death was within her. She must have known it, and it was this mystic knowledge which had inspired and maintained her dark and exquisite gloom.

In this moving passage, Raingo most clearly and most ambiguously reveals the wisdom that lies in the depths of his soul. He lies on the bed exposed—as Henry Earlforward lies on his bed exposed before Dr. Raste. What he knows is anguish. Delphine's " fatal seed " is humanity's: to create is to destroy, to live is to die, to love is to kill, to exalt is to vitiate. Her fatal seed is Raingo's: his desire, jealousy, rage. Her fatal seed may be his child: not in self-punishment for the soldier's death, not in despair of being a lady, not in guilt for her attachment to Gwen, but rather in the agony of pregnancy Delphine may have committed suicide: the evidence of the jury that pronounces her death to be suicide is never mentioned. Raingo kills Delphine and he kills himself. In his heart he does so: Death was in his heart. When the miniature Virgin falls out of his bed (falls as a woman falls, falls as Delphine falls from the cliff in committing suicide), Raingo knows that he will die.

Lord Raingo is often read as a social document. Lafourcade writes that " It is with the ' public life ' of Raingo that
the critic is chiefly concerned," and other critics have paired
the characters with counterparts in life: Andrew Clyth
with Lloyd George, Tom Hogarth with Winston Churchill,
Raingo with Lord Beaverbrook (from whom Bennett obtained much information on governmental affairs for the
novel) and with Lord Rhondda. Bennett himself wrote an
entertaining article on the matter. But the view of the novel
as a social document is inadequate. *Lord Raingo* is a character portrayal that makes use of a particular social scene,
and makes use of it to a much lesser extent than, say, *The
Old Wives' Tale* makes use of a social scene. In the earlier
novel the social scene is important in itself and in its partial
determination of character; in *Lord Raingo* the social scene
is the backdrop—an appropriate, an interesting one—against
which Raingo enacts his tragedy. Frank Swinnerton, Bennett's good friend, has remarked in conversation that Raingo
is a portrait of Arnold Bennett.

Shortly after finishing writing the novel, Bennett wrote
a letter to Swinnerton in which he noted that " the *Saturday
Evening Post* will buy it if they like the last part; but I
know they won't like the last part." He devoted the last
third of the novel to describing a man's dying. Presumably
the editors of the *Post* wanted a social document, modified
to suit the tastes of their market, and they did not buy
Lord Raingo. Bennett saw his artistic task differently: for
him, " the foundation of good fiction is character-creating,
and nothing else."

Lord Raingo is a fine portrait. Not so profound as the
best Conradian or Dostoevskian portraits, and not quite
of the same nature. This image of a mind destroying itself
by desire ("I am mad! I am mad! ") has its own true
quality: a clear surface and clear depths.

CHAPTER 3

Symbol and Image

A MAN FROM THE NORTH
THE OLD WIVES' TALE
THE GLIMPSE

IN HIS BOOK *The Literary Symbol*, W. Y. Tindall points out that there is symbolism to be found in realistic novels. Although he calls Arnold Bennett a novelist of facts rather than of imagination, he acknowledges that such a book as *The Old Wives' Tale* is less literal, more suggestive, than Mrs. Woolf allows it to be. He does not explore the suggestiveness, for he is not concerned with fiction in which symbolism is accidental, occasional, or fragmentary; he mentions the realists simply to set up a contrast with the thoroughgoing symbolists. When he discusses the recurring symbols in *A Portrait of the Artist as a Young Man* or the cave image that is central to *A Passage to India*, he assumes that there are no counterparts in realistic novels. However, Arnold Bennett's symbolism is thoroughgoing.

Bennett himself says almost nothing about symbolism in any of his writing, but his two statements on it of any significance indicate what he intends his own practice to be, and the second identifies one of the two writers who probably influenced him most in regard to it. In a letter to his good friend George Sturt, written in 1896, before he had completed his first novel, he praises the Goncourt's

Germinie Lacerteux because it has " no tortured symbolism of incident." And in *The Author's Craft,* written in 1913, he comments upon Thomas Hardy's " deep conviction of the whimsicality of the divine power " and goes on to assert that " the plot of *The Woodlanders* is one of the most exquisite examples of subtle symbolic illustration of an idea that a writer of fiction ever achieved; it makes the symbolism of Ibsen seem crude."

In remarking upon *The Woodlanders,* Bennett presumably had in mind the two major aspects of its symbolism. The first is the concatenation of fateful chances in the lives of the characters, by which Hardy illustrates his philosophical determinism: Giles Winterborne's losing his house and his betrothed, Grace Melbury, through Mrs. Charmond's chance dislike of him; his losing his hut and his life through Grace's chance renewal of love for him. The second is nature's betrayal of the human heart, by which Hardy illustrates his philosophical pessimism: Giles perishing in the storm at night while " sometimes a bough from an adjoining tree was swayed so low as to smite the roof in the manner of a gigantic hand smiting the mouth of an adversary, to be followed by a trickle of rain, as blood from the wound." Bennett admired Hardy above all other English novelists of the nineteenth and twentieth centuries; he wrote once, " Never in English prose literature was such a seer of beauty as Thomas Hardy." His own philosophical outlook being very close to Hardy's, it is unlikely that he failed to see both the broad and the subtle aspects of the symbolism that pervades *The Woodlanders.* His own symbolism being thoroughgoing, it is unlikely that he failed to learn much from his acquaintance with Hardy's.

Exactly what he learned it is impossible to say. For even when in his novel *Sacred and Profane Love* he plots a chain of fateful chances, his focus is sufficiently different

from Hardy's to cast doubt upon Hardy as his source. The
concluding event of the book, the accidental death of the
heroine just after she has apparently redeemed the life of
her lover, does not illustrate that the universe is malignant
but rather that on occasion it can be—as Bennett explains
in a foreword to the American edition of the book—
" wantonly kind ": the heroine, whose character is her fate,
has been pursuing trouble throughout her life and at the
end is bent unwittingly on some more.

The other writer from whom Bennett probably learned
most about symbolism is Dostoevsky. There is little doubt
that despite reservations about Dostoevsky's technical skill,
Bennett regarded him as the greatest novelist in the world.
He had read his novels in French translations either in the
late 1890's or in the early years of the twentieth century,
certainly before he had written any of his own major novels.
In 1910 he passed a final judgment upon *Clayhanger*, which
he was then writing: " It assuredly isn't within 10 miles
of Dostoevsky." In 1929 he passed a final judgment upon
James Joyce and D. H. Lawrence: they lack the compassion
which is the essential quality of the greatest artist, the artist
such as Dostoevsky. Two years earlier he was reading *The
Brothers Karamazov* for the fourth time, " slowly to savor
it. It is very great and masterful." These comments do
not help to suggest what Bennett's understanding of Dostoevsky's symbolism was; they can only suggest that he responded
to Dostoevsky deeply and read him carefully. The evidence
of his understanding is in his own art, which displays a
similar technique. Dostoevsky builds his symbols in large
part by repeating, with variation, certain actions, scenes,
images, colors, details, until they acquire a significance that
extends beyond the context in which they immediately
appear. Thus in *Crime and Punishment* the color of the
wallpaper in several ugly rooms is yellow, Sonia's prostitute

ticket is yellow, and the faces and clothing of some unhealthy or demoralized people are yellow: the color gradually emerges as a symbol of corruption. Thus the several
depictions of physical assault—Raskolnikov's killing of Aly-
ona, the sexual beatings that Svidrigailov gives Marfa
(whom in the end he possibly kills) , the " author's " beating
of people in the brothel—constitute an image of the ambiguous situation of mankind. (The method contrasts with
that of, say, Flaubert, in his symbolism of the blind tramp
in *Madame Bovary,* or Dickens in his symbolism of the fog
in *Bleak House.*) Presumably Bennett did not learn his
lesson merely from Dostoevsky; he could as well have
learned color symbolism from Stephen Crane, whom he was
reading in the late nineties, and he learned some of it
from the French symbolists. But Dostoevsky was the writer
to whom he was closest; and the novel that he wrote in
1910 that does not come within ten miles of Dostoevsky
is a prime example of a similar technique. It is worth
noting that the basic image of *Clayhanger* is a beating; the
subject of the novel is the same aspect of the oedipal situation with which *The Brothers Karamazov* deals.

Even in his first novel, *A Man from the North,* begun in
1895, Bennett displays some artful symbolism, and in *The
Old Wives' Tale,* completed thirteen years later, he shows
most of the resources that all of his later serious novels
systematically exploit. The former novel develops some
of its symbolism rather too obviously, as in the symboliza-
tion of the hero's failures by a ship's slipping away from
harbor (The method is that of Flaubert, upon whose art
the novel was consciously modelled.) The hero and his
fiancée go down to the quays at Littlemouth and see a ship
at anchor:

His fancy was in the rosy future, vividly picturing the light-

hearted gaieties, Bohemian, unconventional, artistic, in which
he and she should unite.

The hero thinks of declaring his love, but he does not.
The next day, alone, he watches the ship leave. Later he
sits with a less romantic girl on the less romantic Chelsea
Embankment and listens to the splash of oars of a less
romantic rowboat. The new girl is the girl for whom he
will renounce his Bohemian dreams and settle down into
bourgeois respectability: "His ambition floated out of
sight." This time by the water's edge he proposes. The
other girl has sailed for America. In immediately succeeding novels, Bennett's symbolism becomes more complex
and more Dostoevskian; the very next novel, *Anna of the
Five Towns*, marks the clear beginning of Bennett's eventually extensive religious symbolism, and *Sacred and Profane
Love* of four years later explores parallel symbolic actions
with considerable richness. But it is *The Old Wives' Tale*
that provides the first display of real mastery.

Some of the incidental symbolism in *The Old Wives' Tale*
has already been mentioned: the tooth-pulling, the scissors,
the cigar and its ring. Among the more important incidental symbols is that of the cave. It appears most notice-
ably—if it catches the reader's attention at all—as a metaphor
used repeatedly to describe the underground kitchen of the
Baines household, the place where the servant spends her
day: "Maggie's cavern-home." Subsequent references to
the kitchen are frequently in the following manner: "Amy
Bates [a successor to Maggie], still inhabiting the cave."
The metaphor, plain and amusing, seems merely to comment upon social caste, to imply a view of servants as
animals lower than human beings. (Bennett remarks elsewhere in the novel on the seventeen-hour day, seven-day
week, with one day off a month, that Maggie gives to the
Baineses; and in the opening scene of the novel Constance

and Sophia laugh at Maggie's pretense of civilized love.)
But it relates to other images and extends its meaning.

In Book Two young Cyril Povey commits two crimes.
After the first one he hides himself in the second of two
cellars that lie behind the underground kitchen and are
reached by an underground passage; he is thought by his
parents to be lost. Some years later he hides some illicit
purchases in the same cellar, and is betrayed by the cavern-
dwelling servant. At the end of the novel, when Constance
is dying, " in all her delirium she was invariably wandering
to and fro in the long underground passage leading from
the scullery past the coal-cellar and the cinder-cellar to the
backyard. And she was afraid of the vast-obscure of those
regions, as she had been in her infancy." These lines recall
Sophia's delirium in Paris. Sophia is " lying in bed in a
small room, obscure . . . ," and in her delirium " she was
. . . in a watery gulf, terribly deep. . . . Hands seized her
and forced her from the subaqueous grotto where she had
hidden. . . ." Both of these imaginings are prepared for
by a single early reference in the novel to Constance and
Sophia's childhood feelings about the cellar regions of the
Baines house: " the sense of the vast-obscure of those regions . . . , a sense which Constance and Sophia had acquired
in infancy, remained with them almost unimpaired as they
grew old."

These several images of the cellars relate to crime, fear,
and secrecy. Other metaphors and related images expand
the implications. In the opening scene of the novel Sophia
tries on her mother's hoop skirt and falls over in it; the
largest ring of the hoop looks " like a cavern's mouth."
Samuel Povey's mouth appears to Sophia, as she prepares
to pull his tooth, like a " cavern " in which the gale of
his respiration blows. When young Cyril at his party discovers that his precious cake is being consumed by other

people, "his tiny mouth grew and grew, like a mouth in a nightmare." When Sophia and Gerald have a secret ren- dezvous in the country, they see "a raw gash in the earth; and hundreds of men . . . crawling about in it . . . the curse of a God-fearing and respectable district! . . . dangerous beasts of prey. . . ." (The image suggests Hell, although the men are merely creating a new railway.) A few minutes later Sophia and Gerald come upon an abandoned shaft. In Sophia's mind arise "dreadful images of the ghosts of miners wandering forever in subterranean passages, far, far beneath. . . . She could scarcely even look at the wall without a spasm of fear." Against her wishes Gerald climbs the wall of the pit, looks in, and reports to her, "No bottom to be seen!" Immediately thereupon Sophia becomes angry with him and turns and runs off. Presumably, Gerald is looking into the bottomless pit of sin and hell; and Sophia, who has recently heard a sermon in which the pit was luridly described, is rejecting the implicit invitation to look into the pit with him. (The scene foreshadows her refusal to stay in London with him without being married.) In Book Two the newly married Constance and Samuel pre- pare to go to bed together in the Baines home for the first time. Constance chances to make a disparaging remark about Samuel's paper collars, and Samuel becomes angry. A quarrel threatens momentarily. "Both of them suddenly saw that they were standing on the edge of a chasm, and drew back. They had imagined themselves to be wandering safely in a flowering meadow, and here was this bottomless chasm!" Constance when she is giving birth to Cyril feels herself "at the edge of the precipice."

Other similar metaphors in the novel refer to secret thoughts and feelings: Mrs. Baines knows nothing of the "bright lamps burning in . . . mysterious grottoes and caverns of the brain" of daughter Sophia; Gerald, bent

upon possessing Sophia, "kept saying to himself, far off
in some remote cavern of the brain: 'I shall have her!'"
and so forth. The several things that all these metaphors
and related images concern are secret feelings, physical
agony, sin, hell and the tortures of hell, sexuality, secret
action, fear, and crime. Their general implication is
summed up in Sophia's thought when she saves her boarding house in the Rue Bréda from being burned down
accidentally by Chirac, who possibly has intended to commit suicide: "That humanity walks ever on a thin crust
over terrific abysses." This metaphor is all-encompassing,
embracing even the metaphors of the kitchen-cave. It refers
to the abysses of the unconscious mind beneath the conscious; and it refers to the social and evolutionary abysses
beneath the Baines household, the kitchen-cave where labors
a servant, a "dehumanized drudge," and thence the gullies
and mines where labor "the curse of a God-fearing and
respectable district! . . . dangerous beasts. . . ." Constance
and Sophia ask themselves in the opening scene of the
novel as they watch the servant Maggie take her monthly
airing: "Why should she want to stir out of her kitchen?"
The answer is simply that Maggie wants to be a human
being too; and over the course of the novel a quiet social
revolution takes place, so that by the time Sophia and
Constance are old women together again in Bursley their
difficulties in retaining a servant at all force them temporarily to abandon the house, and the open impertinence
of the servant Maud makes them feel "as though they had
glimpsed the end of civilized society." That their viewpoint is narrow and their superiority relative is clear
enough: they live in the caves of their own minds, and
they and their social equals live in crude houses and sometimes in fact live in the cellars of those houses. Bennett
remarks in the Paris chapters that at one point during the

Commune the whole population of Paris lived in the cellars (in French: *caves*). When Sophia first returns to Bursley from Paris she finds the whole Baines house "extremely inconvenient, dark, and no doubt unhealthy. Cellar-kitchen, no hall, abominable stairs, and as to hygiene, simply medieval."

Although the symbol of the cave plays a minor role, its significance relates it to the major symbol of the novel: the execution of the berserk elephant in Book One. Executions are designed to control uprisings from psychological and social caves (from the beast in man); sometimes instead they cause such uprisings. Bennett is primarily concerned in the novel with the latter situation, and the execution of the beast is his principal symbol. The elephant, one of the animals at the Bursley Wakes, gores a man, providing "the greatest sensation that has ever occurred, or perhaps ever will occur, in Bursley." It is formally executed: bound, made to kneel, and shot by members of the Rifle Corps while crowds of people look on excitedly. The excutioners are borne off triumphantly to various inns and the body is later assaulted—tusks, feet, and flesh—for souvenirs. These upheavals are minor. The elephant is responsible for the major upheavals of the novel. Because the Baineses go out to watch its execution, their shop is left unattended, and Sophia, who has remained behind to care for bedridden John Baines, has to leave him to go into the shop to wait on Gerald Scales. John Baines ("Mid-Victorian England") falls out of bed and is asphyxiated; his death marks the beginning of upheavals in morals and caste: Sophia abandoning home and honor to pursue Gerald; Constance marrying beneath the family dignity, marrying a clerk, who, snubbed during Baines's life, gradually assumes control of the shop. The elephant is John Baines, the elephant is mid-Victorian England; the two deaths occur in the same

chapter, entitled " Elephant "; and at the elaborate funeral
tea following John Baines's death, " the elephant fed the
conversation "—like a proper god or totem. (Sophia, who
is the only person absent from the totemic feast, nevertheless gets her portion: years later during the siege of Paris
she eats elephant soup.)

In each of the three other books of the novel there occurs
a formal execution that is marked by great upheavals or
indicates such upheavals, and that is responsible for another
major death. In Book Two Daniel Povey is executed for
murdering his drunken wife. The circumstances being
extenuating, local citizens believe that Daniel is " judicially
murdered," but at his hearing the behavior of the crowd
and the police is " as though the crowd had yelled for
Daniel's blood and bones, and the faithful constables saved
him from their lust." Immediately following the memorial
ceremony for him there are the same " funereal thirst " and
" orgy " that accompany the deaths of the elephant and
John Baines. The attendant death is that of Samuel Povey,
who wears himself out and dies trying to save Daniel from
the gallows. In Book Three occurs the execution to which
Bennett gives closest attention, the guillotining of Rivain
that Sophia and Gerald witness. The unseemly eating and
drinking and promiscuous sexual activity that accompany
the event are Bennett's most explicit presentation of his
theme. The event is an occasion for the celebration of
lusts. There are interesting similarities in the details of the
descriptions of the three executions: Rivain is pictured
" between two warders, who pressed against him "; Daniel
is seen as " a sort of Christ between two thieves," the thieves
being policemen; and the dead elephant, " by the help
of his two companions," fellow elephants, is lifted into a
railroad lorry. The death attending Rivain's is Gerald's
sexual death. Before the execution " he had been proudly

conversing with impudent women. Now, in swift collapse, he was as flaccid as a sick hound." His metaphorical death points to the death of his relationship with Sophia, which, when it formally occurs in the next chapter, results in Sophia's illness. Rivain's execution also relates to the most obvious social upheaval in the novel, the upheaval of French society in the Franco-Prussian war, the subject of the succeeding chapter.

In Book Four occurs the last of the executions; it is a metaphorical execution, whose significance most closely relates to the symbolical execution of the elephant; it is the judicial murder of Bursley via federation. Bennett's language can be understood to suggest a guillotining: " there were actually people who wished to bow the neck to Hanbridge " (the town advocating federation). The execution does not take place within the novel; it is temporarily staved off; but " as a center of commerce it [Bursley] had assuredly approached very near death "; and Charles Critchlow remarks at the funeral of Constance, who had died of a cold she caught in going out to vote again federation (like Samuel in going out to fight against Daniel's execution), " It's a pity her didn't live long enough to hear as Federation is going on after all! That would ha' worritted her."

The social upheaval involved in execution via federation is the final destruction of the world that John Baines represents. Although mid-Victorian England dies with him, his shop remains and much of the Victorian code remains: the real heir to his shop marries his daughter and conducts his business with Victorian conscientiousness, and even though Sophia as a girl flouts Victorian morality, she later becomes the very symbol of virtue and enterprise. The death of Bursley, though, is the death of the Baines shop; it passes into the hands of a modern chain store. The death of Bursley brings the death of Constance and an end to the Baines family in Bursley; for Sophia has already died; and Constance's only son—a dilettante rather than a man of stern virtues—has left the area permanently.

The death of the elephant is the symbol of a three-act tragedy: the first act presents the death of mid-Victorian England, the breaking down of moral and social codes in the household of John Baines following his death; the second presents a rearguard action in Bursley and Paris; the third brings about the dissolution of the Victorian world under the pressures of a new society. (The tragedy ends like a Shakespearean tragedy, with the suggestion of new life.) Contrasting with the three-act tragedy of English society is the tragedy in one act: the crisis of French society. It is in terms of these tragedies that all of Bennett's patient, realistic details about changes in dress over the years, replacement of oil light by gas light, etc., must be understood. They are not merely observed facts.

In the light of the psychological theme of the novel, the death of the elephant suggests the intricate connections between death and life. The elephant is killed at the scene of a carnival, and its death feeds the carnival spirit. All of the other executions, and many of the minor deaths in the novel, are attended by similar outbursts of vitality. At the same time, death brings death: the death of the elephant is responsible for the death of John Baines, and the other executions bring other deaths. This latter implication is especially clear in the climactic death scene of the novel, Sophia's confrontment of the dead body of Gerald Scales toward the end of Book Four. Three times in her life Sophia has seen a dead man. On the first occasion, when she discovers her dead father, she runs out of the room and then runs away from home to life. On the second occasion, when she watches the guillotining, she says to herself, " I

cannot stand this," but she does, at the cost of being transformed from a lively young girl into the "tragic masterpiece" of her mature years. On this third occasion when
she confronts Gerald, she virtually repeats her earlier words,
saying, "I cannot stand it," and she dies.

One of Bennett's ironies that only an analysis of the
novel's hidden chronology discloses is that ten years earlier
Sophia predicts her death to within a month. In the agony
of her having been discovered at the Pension Frensham by
Matthew Peel-Swinnerton, she thinks to herself: "It was
appalling—the passage of years; and the passage of years
would grow more appalling. Ten years hence, where would
she be? She pictured herself dying."

Once Bennett's symbolism becomes clear, the perspective
in which *The Old Wives' Tale* is seen must be shifted.
E. M. Forster's remark, in *Aspects of the Novel*, that "time
is the real hero" no longer seems entirely adequate. He
writes:

> Sophia and Constance are the children of Time from the
> instant we see them romping with their mother's dresses;
> they are doomed to decay with a completeness that is very
> rare in literature. They are girls, Sophia runs away and
> marries, the mother dies, Constance marries, her husband
> dies, Sophia's husband dies, Sophia dies, Constance dies,
> their old rheumatic dog lumbers up to see whether anything
> remains in the saucer. Our daily life in time is exactly this
> business of getting old. . . . But a great book must rest on
> something more than an "of course," and *The Old Wives'
> Tale* is strong, sincere, sad, it misses greatness.

The title of Book Four of the novel is "What Life Is,"
and on Forster's terms Bennett means that life consists of
growing old and dying. But the final image of the book,
Sophia's old dog Fossette going on unsteady legs to her
supper while Constance is being buried, symbolizes more

than this. It " of course " suggests that the Baines family
and French culture leave no more impress upon Bursley,
no more trace, than an old unshorn French poodle lapping
its supper; it also suggests, as does the main symbolic beast
in the novel, that life renews itself in the very moments
of death.* The renewal here is feeble, ironic, in keeping
with Bennett's focus: he is ending his novel in a minor key,
he has made his subject much more the dissolution of the
old than the emergence of the new, much more Bursley's
dying than the birth of the federated city. Fossette's going
to her supper symbolizes life-in-death. (Such meaning is
distinct from the meaning which surrounds the fact that
" what life is " for Sophia is different from what it is for
Constance. For Sophia it is monstrous; for Constance it is
prosaic.)

E. M. W. Tillyard's description of the novel as a celebration of provincial life seems more appropriate. One might
want to say that it is a celebration not of provincial life
but of life itself—a celebration in death. Constance in voting
against federation fails to see " the cosmic movement in
large curves "; it is this movement that Bennett sees and
epitomizes in the execution of the elephant and in all of
the other transfiguring deaths.

Complex and subtle though the symbolism in *The Old
Wives' Tale* is (there are many minor symbols in it comparable to the cave symbol), it does not display the full
imaginative coherence that the symbolism of Bennett's later
novels characteristically does. The elephant is assuredly
an appropriate symbol of Victorian England, representing

---

* In a dissertation that he is writing at the University of Illinois,
Thomas E. Coleman discusses in some detail the animal imagery in
the novel. Mr. Coleman has also independently noticed the four
executions that unite the four books of the novel.

well the essential qualities of ponderosity and empire; and the burden with which it is loaded is never artistically excessive: the elephant remains an elephant belonging to the Wombwell Circus, and the novel remains a novel about life rather than becoming a novel about symbols of life. Nevertheless, the elephant is not a very suggestive symbol, it does not extend its meanings, it does not relate imaginatively to the other symbols in the novel. Insofar as Bennett was free to choose his symbols, he might have chosen better. The elephant does not stand very well alone, and it does not belong in Bennett's cave.

In his immediately succeeding serious novel, *The Glimpse*, Bennett develops his symbolism with much greater imaginative skill. The major symbol, a mirror (suggested in the title), identifies itself with the theme of the novel, the characters, and the action; and it is the direct source of all of the minor symbols or is related to them in an intimate way. Some of the symbolism springs from the theosophy upon which the novel is ostensibly based, some of it springs from a more mundane source, Bennett's friendship with Maurice Ravel. Such is the use of friendship to a realistic novelist.

Something should be said beforehand about Bennett's viewpoint with regard to the subject of the novel, whose central event is the experience the hero undergoes after he has supposedly died. Bennett was an agnostic. He despised formal religion with great passion, and he considered intellectual discussion of such subjects as immortality an unprofitable pursuit. Nevertheless, he refused to reject the possibility of supernatural experience, and he dealt with it imaginatively time and again. One of his earliest novels, *The Ghost*, treats the ghost of a dead man as though it were a real thing rather than a product of the hero's imagination. Some of his short stories deal with paracognition, as do

two of his later novels, *The Pretty Lady*, which is one of
his best novels, and the unfinished *Dream of Destiny*.

In *The Glimpse* Bennett presents the supernatural experience in such a way that the reader can take it as a true
experience or as a fantasy. The hero, who is the narrator,
relates his experience with full belief in its objective
validity, and Bennett questions that validity only indirectly:
what the hero sees in his experience after death may be
a fantasy that stems from his looking at himself in a mirror
as he lies near death; what he hears in his experience may
be a distortion of the sound of the clock in the hall. Bennett
drew the details of his hero's experience from theosophical
writings; the core of the plot, the return to life of a man
presumed to be dead, he drew from a dream he himself
once had and from an account of such an experience given
him by a friend. At the time of writing the novel, Bennett
remarked that there was a lot of autobiographical material
in it; and although he was dissatisfied with the section of
the book dealing with the hero's experience after death,
he thought that the rest of the book was " as good as the
best I can do." It is worth remarking that the hero, rather
than Bennett, holds initial responsibility for his literary
manner. Critics who have been put off by the novel seem
in part to have reacted against the false elegance of the
hero's style. Of course Bennett is ultimately responsible
for his hero; and perhaps he does not succeed in disengaging
himself from the arrogant esthete that his hero is. But
that he meant to is indicated by a remark that he made
about *Sacred and Profane Love*, which he chose to narrate
through an hysterical female writer: " The style of the
following pages is not my style; it is the style of Carlotta
Peel."

The novel deals with fundamental matters. Its theme is
desire: desire that leads to evolution, perfection, and disso-

lution; egotistical desire and sympathetic desire that lead
to isolation and union, to evolution, perfection, and dissolution. Morrice Loring, the narrator and hero, is a dilettante intellectual and art connoisseur whose mind has
evolved to a degree of perfection that isolates him from
most of humanity: " I had the consciousness of immense
and successful endeavor, of being unsurpassed in my
sphere "; he has " won renown among the disdainers of the
multitude." His wife, Inez, is the epitome of sensual and
brilliant womanhood: " The whole of her life was an evolution of one grace out of another. . . . Inez . . . lived for
pleasure, was a marvelous instrument of pleasure." Contrasting to Loring is Johnnie Hulse, equally the disdainful
art connoisseur but a possessor of great vitality, an artist,
and a connoisseur of women. Contrasting to Inez is Mary
Dean, Loring's sister and a widow, who has refined decor-
ousness and rationalism to an extreme.

The action of the novel presents the conflict and attain-
ment of desire among these people. First, Inez, driven by
an appetite for sensual pleasure and personal attention that
her elegant and self-centered husband cannot appease, seeks
fulfillment with Hulse, who is Loring's close friend. Secondly, Loring, whose more refined desires have brought
him to ennui, seeks to revive his love for his wife: " Far,
far within my soul, the real Me existed still desolate, but
resolutely saying to itself: ' You must learn to live. Perhaps
the whole secret of your despair lies in the fact that, having
once loved ardently, you had ceased to love.' " The collision
of their two desires, through Inez's accidental revelation of
her affair, produces a heart attack in Loring and his " death,"
and thence remorse in Inez and her suicide. As a consequence of his experience Loring evolves and seeks to perfect
a new attitude of compassion toward people. " Nothing
else, beside the perfecting of this attitude had importance."

In the opening scene of the novel, Loring is at a concert
to hear Ravel's *Miroirs*. He assumes that he is one of the
few persons there who are capable of appreciating this new
and perfect music; and he assumes that one day this music
will become acceptable to the crass multitude and will be
supplanted by a new perfection. His attitude defines his
estheticism and his egotism. One of the Philistines at the
concert passes judgment on Loring in passing judgment on
the music. " Morbid! " the man says. As Loring leaves
the concert he sees an elegant woman, whose physical and
material display represent to him another kind of perfection (like his wife's), and passing through Bond Street
he looks through the shop windows at the goods that feed
vanity and enable one to " identify . . . one's self." When
he arrives home, he sees his wife, whom he calls " Mrs.
Conceit," sitting before her toilet mirror. Later that evening, Inez accidentally discloses her affair with Hulse, just
when Loring is trying to offer her his own love again.
Taking the revelation with superficial calm, Loring looks
at himself in a mirror, wondering whether his face reveals
his morbid feelings. A few minutes later, when he has his
heart attack and thinks he is dying, he calls for his mirror
and gazes at his image: " the poor, drawn, beaten, condemned, undignified figure." Surrendering to death, he
thinks of a man lost in Alpine snows: " behold there my
image." Book One ends with this phrase.

In Book Two, Loring finds himself looking at his presumably dead body on the bed—not quite from the mirror
but from a surviving gaseous part of himself that floats
over the bed. He then undergoes several experiences. In
this state he commands a view of myriad flats, hotel rooms,
and barracks in London, all prison-like and yet homelike
" by their human familiarity." He feels " in the most
desperate need of sympathy," " solitary . . . cut off—by an

impassible . . . barrier." He thereupon loses his egotistical disdain of the masses who live in those flats and hotel rooms: "no, not even a gloved lackey, with whom I would not have exchanged lots." Secondly, he discovers that the physical world is transparent and ethereal. The isolation of one person from another, imprisoned in flesh and separated by walls, is an illusion of worldly life. He sees thoughts emanate from his servant to visit her lover; he sees the objects in his room to be part of a " transparent prismatic quivering sea "; he receives sympathetic vibrations of thoughts from Inez. Now he realizes how unjust was his egotistical disdain in life: "Now I knew that a complete physical vision of even a porter . . . would dazzle my sight and my intellect."

He passes thence into an experience of perfect fulfillment of desire, possessing a woman who " had every fine quality in greater profusion than I had met . . . in any woman before "; possessing a library in which " I spent an eternity making contacts with all cultures, and acquiring an erudition that by the standard of an earthly plane would be deemed immeasurable "; and possessing the arts similarly to enjoy. These experiences are a perfect recapitulation of his life, and like a mirror-image they are self-created, egotistical: "I myself had created those instruments to the realization of desire. The woman . . . the literature . . . the works of art. . . . The order of the universe was such that terrific energies of creation were in subject to my impulses." He then realizes that he is in Hell, that Hell is the fulfillment, the completion, the perfection, of egotistical desire, that Hell is self-created. Desire dies, and this physical vision vanishes.

In his final experience, in which he is certain that he is dead physically, he feels that "I was in life. I knew the real." The experience culminates in the dissolution of his individuality, in a union of his mind and instinct, and in a merging of multitudinous previous incarnations of himself. Life and reality, he sees, consist of recurring incarnations in a vast evolutionary arc. Incarnations, involving egotism and isolation, succeed one another, followed by dissolutions, involving sympathy and union. His reincarnations are images of one another: "But as the remoter part swam towards me in the vision, the development of that prisoner [various incarnations of himself] showed unmistakable. . . . I could see him held fast in the grossness of bodies whose crude savagery would have shocked Morrice Loring into inanition" (as his crude sexual feeling for Inez perhaps shocks him). He sees that his egotism in life was disdain of humanity, of individual and social evolution, hence of himself. Just at the moment when, presumably, he would in fact become dead physically, he is summoned back into life by the sound of a gong (the clock in the hall). The succeeding events of the novel show him putting into practice, as best he can, what he has learned. He cannot escape the egotism, the isolation, that flesh engenders, but he can exert himself to be sympathetic and compassionate toward other people.

The symbolic significance of the mirror becomes apparent. Thematically, the mirror refers to the repeated image in reincarnation, to the repeated process of evolution, to the repetition of life in death. As a character symbol, the mirror suggests estheticism (a particular pose toward Ravel's *Miroirs*), self-love, morbidity, perfectionism, imitativeness. (Inez's worst fault, according to Loring, is her "imitativeness." In a more generous mood he says, "she reflected me more quickly than a mirror." The woman in his perfect experience when he is dying "reflected but was not a glass.") In terms of action, the mirror refers to desire, desire for the perfect image, desire for perfection, desire for death; the mirror is the image to be achieved, maintained, broken, repeated. It is from Loring's decision at the Ravel concert to change his life, to break his image, that the action of the novel stems; it is from his contemplation of his broken image in the mirror after his heart attack that the substance of Book Two stems: "the eyes," says the doctor, after Loring has looked at himself in the mirror, "are turned upward, like into the forehead."

A mirror reflects light, of which there are two extremes, light that is broken down into its several colors and light that consists of all colors conjoined. The breaking down of light, the isolation of colors, is achieved by refraction, as occurs when the sun shines to produce a rainbow or when a beam of light is cast through a prism. The union of colors produces white light. In *The Glimpse*, color signifies isolation, egotism, and life; and white light signifies union, sympathy, and death. At the concert Loring thinks of the musical importance of the *Miroirs* as "another step . . . towards . . . the ultimate conquest of a refractory medium." Inez's real name is Iris, suggesting the Greek goddess of the rainbow. Loring thinks that "the room was brightest over her [Inez's] head" and that "Mary could never shine with that radiance." In his experience of dying, when he discerns the gaseous forms that surround people and emanate from them, "the transparent prismatic quivering sea," Loring distinguishes meanings in colors: vivid red is jealous hatred; violet is sexual desire; and a much paler hue, a rose color, is human sympathy. The succeeding experience of the perfection of desire brings him the woman "more radiant than any radiant creature I had yet seen" and the palace "glittering prismatically." In his final experience, in which he moves toward worldly death and toward the primordial union, he sees "white . . . utterly different from the white of snow. . . . A world not of color" and then

" an increase of light; till light seemed gradually to become the absence of light."

The identified parts of the *Miroirs* at the concert are " Night Moths," " Mournful Birds," " The Valley of Bells," and " A Bark on the Ocean." These play a role in the novel subsidiary to the mirror but nevertheless important. " A Bark on the Ocean " is particularly interesting because it changes its significance in the course of the novel to reflect Loring's shift from egotism to compassion. At an early point in the novel, Loring thinks of his home in the following fashion. " The waves of the immense sea of London dashed against the walls of my fortress; but within the fortress . . . my egotism had established silence and calm." He regards a taxicab which, he thinks, is bearing two egotists into a love affair as " a boat . . . [in] the middle of the Square," a boat in which they are " imprisoned." In the second section of the novel, the image is first used to suggest loneliness and the dissolution of individuality. Loring thinks of himself as " a sailor marooned on a desert islet "; later he sees himself as " a ship that, determined not to fly before the wind, slides across it." The ocean itself is " solitude." Then occurs Loring's rebirth, when he believes he is being reincarnated and when the transformation from egotism to compassion becomes fixed. The image of the bark on the ocean now suggests immersion, companionship, and love. Loring describes his rebirth in the following image. " When the swimmer unclothes, and abandons himself to the water, naked, letting the water caress the whole of his nakedness . . . , then . . . the thought occurs to him that to love otherwise than in that naked freedom is not to love." In Book Three the new meaning becomes clear. Loring, revived, sees that he must conduct his life unselfishly, he must live for others: " I would yield myself to them utterly as to the water of a tide; I would live in them." In the closing scene of the novel, the image becomes a reality, when Loring is in an actual boat that is carrying him from France to England; it is then given the broadest thematic significance. Loring is on the boat with the child Edith, his niece, toward whom he has had his first real opportunity to display compassion—by comforting her tenderly when she breaks a valuable vase; and at the end of the voyage, which is very rough, he carries her in his arms onto shore. He himself sees the bark not merely as a voyaging ship but also as a voyaging soul; and when he comes to land he sees the bark as the English island in the sea and as the human situation: "I . . . had the sensation of being on an island insecurely anchored in a great sea. We were all huddled together on that bit of turf that raised its breast from the sea to encounter the winds; and we were doing what we could; and we called the episode life."

The other parts of the *Miroirs* are developed with like complexity. And they, along with the chief symbol, the mirror, are related to two subsidiary groups of symbols: window-veil-wall-refuge-prison-palace and glass-vase-cup-flower. Some of these symbols have appeared in the preceding discussion, and there is no need to explore them except to remark that they too either shift in implication in the course of the novel or else substitute for each other appropriately. The prison symbolizes Loring's self-isolation and egotism in Book One, and symbolizes any human incarnation in Book Three. The vase, a precious art work, symbolizes Loring's estheticism and his brittle heart and soul; it is broken in the course of the novel. A cup and saucer replace it on the mantelpiece; they symbolize the mundane sympathy that Loring has learned.

The symbolism in *The Glimpse*, is complex, imaginative, and coherent. From the title, from the opening scene at the Ravel concert, to the last line of the novel, Bennett elaborates it. At the very end he needs only an oblique reference to a mirror image to sum up the novel. Loring has learned compassion; he has committed himself to a new evolution, a new perfection. In the last two sentences he describes his situation and his experience: " I was alone. But I had seen God." That is to say, he has looked inward at himself (as when he looked in the mirror when he was dying) and by doing so he has looked outward; his glimpse of himself is his glimpse of the universe; his contemplation of himself is the source of his compassion. One should not ignore the irony of the passage: the mirror image is a vain, anthropomorphic image. At the same time, the image is an ennobled one. If the reader rejects the objective validity of the experience Loring undergoes, he sees traces of the arrogant esthete in Loring's final words. (Not, as some critics have thought, a statement of Bennett's own outlook on life.) Nevertheless, Loring becomes a new man—within psychological limits—by his subjective experience.

Although Bennett's critics do not agree about his viewpoint toward the subject of *The Glimpse*, they are generally agreed that it is a poor and freakish work. It is not one of his very best novels, but it has many fine passages and scenes. The image with which Loring expresses his agony of dying, " the freezing blast that moans in the hollow between two worlds nipped me, and I was naked to it," and the very tender scene in which Loring comforts his niece after she has broken his precious vase are Bennett at his best. Moreover, the novel is basically characteristic of Bennett. Though the one-to-one relationship of the facts of the novel to certain external facts of life is less significant than in other novels, Bennett does draw Morrice Loring's first name and something of his character from Maurice

Ravel; he does in the fourth chapter provide a detailed description of Bond Street; and he does acknowledge in his *Journal* that there is a considerable autobiographical element in the novel. More importantly, the theme of *The Glimpse* is the paramount theme of all of his novels, and the technique is his characteristic technique. The theme is—to choose another word than desire—evolution, which has been shown to be the theme of *The Old Wives' Tale* and which will be seen to be the dominating theme of most of the other novels. And the unfolding symbolism is the characteristic technique of the later novels: the presentation of a scene or image at the outset that contains the major symbols and that all subsequent scenes or images reflect.

CHAPTER 4

Symbol, Image, and Reality

CLAYHANGER

BENNETT ONCE WROTE, "If I could choose an epitaph for my grave it would be: 'He tried to destroy illusions.'" There is no epitaph on his grave; there is not even the right death date. He does have a literary epitaph; it is Gradgrindian: "Now, what I want is, Facts." Henry James was the first important critic to pronounce it. Bennett, says James in *Notes on Novelists*, possesses exhaustive information on his subject and produces his work simply by squeezing the orange of his information, the juice thereof being the theme. (The metaphor is James's.) Other artists rely on passion, imagination, and inspiration; Bennett relies on information. Unfortunately, James concludes, the resulting work, such as *The Old Wives' Tale* or *Clayhanger*, lacks line, composition, and purpose. Imagine, then, James's astonishment when Bennett denied possessing his only capacity. Bennett recorded the moment in his *Journal*: "Henry James at Pinker's. Very slow talker. Beautiful French. Expressed stupefaction when I said I knew nothing about the middle class, and said the next time he saw me he would have recovered from the stupefaction, and the conversation might proceed." It is interesting that another fellow writer, the Jamesian Ford Madox Ford, could say that of all the English authors he knew, Bennett alone loved to discuss literary technique.

The lie has been given to James's viewpoint. The analysis of *The Old Wives' Tale* in the previous chapter, partial though it is, makes clear the imaginative and technical resources by which Bennett gave his facts line, composition, and purpose. But it is not enough to say that Bennett does marshal his facts very neatly, does make them do a dance, does transform them into symbols, does weave the symbols into a design. He is, when all is said and done, a realist in the most serious sense of the term; he is preoccupied with the realities of the human situation. He would never have been contented with an art, however clever its line, composition, and purpose, that was mainly fanciful. When he says of Henry James that " in the fastidiousness of his taste he rather repudiated life," he is judging the artist as well as the man. His symbolism at its best, at its most character-istic, serves his realism.

It can be said of the elephant in *The Old Wives' Tale* that however aptly it is chosen to symbolize mid-Victorian England, it is first and last (and in a sense admirably so) an animal that happens to be in a carnival at Bursley; its presence is one of the miscellaneous provincial facts of life that Bennett chooses rather than rejects, and imposes his burden upon. Contrastingly, it can be said of the mirror in *The Glimpse* that however firmly it is placed in the real world, it is first and last (admirably too) an imaginative thematic device; the nature of Loring's fantasy as he lies near death does not derive in a valid psychological way from the fact that he has just held a mirror in his hand. What the elephant and the mirror have in common is that they justify themselves in limited esthetic terms, satisfying on the one hand the convention of realism and on the other the demand for thematic unity; they do not possess appro-priateness or inevitability in a broad extra-artistic sense. In contrast, the symbolism in *Clayhanger* and in some of the later novels justifies itself to a considerable extent in terms of Bennett's philosophical understanding of the relationship between the world of external appearances and actualities and the world of the mind, an understanding which he sets forth in his slender book about his art, *The Author's Craft*.

Appropriately enough, the book begins not with a formal analysis of the author's craft but with a chapter on " Seeing Life," in which Bennett describes a random event on a London street, a dog being run over, and discusses its ramifications. Before a novelist becomes a novelist, he sees life, sees innumerable incidents which he sorts out, classifies, gives meanings to, explains, according to his analytical and synthetic powers and according to his understanding of the nature of life. When the novelist writes, he sees life similarly and expresses what he has seen. Bennett then proceeds to explain in broad terms how he himself has seen and understood life. He begins with externals:

> Any logically conceived survey of existence must begin with geographical and climatic phenomena. This is surely obvious. If you say that you are not interested in meteorology or the configurations of the earth, I say that you deceive yourself. You are. For an east wind may upset your liver and cause you to insult your wife. Beyond question the most important fact about, for example, Great Britain is that it is an island. . . . In moments of journalistic vainglory we are apt to refer to the "sturdy island race," meaning us. But that we are insular in the full significance of the horrid word is certain. Why not? A genuine observation of the supreme phenomenon that Great Britain is surrounded by water—an effort to keep it always at the back of the consciousness—will help to explain all the minor phenomena of British existence.

What is most significant about Bennett's viewpoint is that

he does not consider the external facts of life—geographical and climatic phenomena—to be interesting in themselves but rather in relationship to human mentality. He sees the external world impinging upon the internal world, not explaining it but helping to explain it. For such a reason he puts Constance and Sophia Baines on the fifty-third parallel and gives the geography of Staffordshire. The quality he attributes to England he attributes to a greater degree to the Five Towns: "It is England in little, lost in the midst of England"; if the geographical position of England accounts in part for the English people, so the position of the Five Towns accounts in part for the Baineses. (In a psychoanalytic essay—published, ironically enough, by the Hogarth Press—Ernest Jones derives the English national character from the physical insularity of the British Isles.)

Bennett then establishes a second order of externals, those which not only influence mentality but are influenced by it:

> Geographical knowledge is the mother of discernment, for the varying physical characteristics of the earth are the sole direct terrestrial influence determining the evolution of original vital energy.
>
> All other influences are secondary, and have been effects of character and temperament before becoming causes.

Among secondary causes, he says, "perhaps the greatest . . . are roads and architecture." Had he been more prescient than he was, he might have added Mrs. Woolf's railway carriage. Of Edwin Clayhanger, a young man with artistic impulses, Bennett writes:

> In that head of his a flame burnt that was like an altar-fire, a miraculous and beautiful phenomenon, than which nothing is more miraculous nor more beautiful over the whole earth. Whence had it suddenly sprung, that flame? . . .

It bursts forth out of a damp jungle of careless habits and negligence that could not possibly have fed it. There is little to encourage it. The very architecture of the streets shows that environment has done naught for it: ragged brick-work, walls finished anyhow with saggers and slag; narrow uneven alleys leading to higgledy-piggledy workshops. . . .

Bennett is not accounting for Edwin in terms of the external facts of life. Yet it is an external fact of life—the Georgian façade of the Sytch Pottery—that provides the moment for Edwin's flame to burn most brightly. In the touching scene in which he is shown the façade by the architect Orgreave, who regards it as the sole beautiful architectural work in the Five Towns, Edwin decides to defy his father and become an architect. He does not succeed, and the ugliness of most of the architecture in the Five Towns accounts in part for his failure. Yet Edwin's mind is superior to the minds that produced the "higgledy-piggledy worshops," and it reflects its quality as they reflected theirs: he builds in his maturity (in the third novel of the trilogy, *These Twain*) a new shop to replace his father's ugly one. And the more propitious external world that he helps to create may be considered in part responsible for the fact that his foster son does indeed become the architect that he failed to be. (The novel *The Roll-Call*, which concerns the foster son, is fairly closely related to the trilogy of *Clayhanger*, *Hilda Lessways*, and *These Twain*.)

Bennett, then, is concerned with the external world in its relationship to human mentality. His final words on the subject in *The Author's Craft* are clear:

Every street is a mirror, an illustration, an exposition, an explanation, of the human beings who live in it. Nothing in it is to be neglected. Everything in it is valuable, if the perspective is maintained. Nevertheless, in the narrow individualistic novels of English literature—and in some of the best—you will find a domestic organism described as though it existed in a vacuum, or in the Sahara, or between Heaven and earth; as though it reacted on nothing and was reacted on by nothing; and as though it could be adequately rendered without reference to anything exterior to itself. How can such novels satisfy a reader who has acquired or wants to acquire the faculty of seeing life?

Bennett's whole point in *The Author's Craft* is perhaps an obvious one. Few people would deny it. At the same time it is an elusive point, difficult to grasp imaginatively and difficult to elucidate. Even if one acknowledges that Mrs. Woolf is wrong in denying the relevance of the railway carriage to the soul of Mrs. Brown, one may nevertheless be suspicious that among many realists the description of the carriage does represent an evasion of her soul. To show that the iron has entered the soul of Mrs. Brown, to show that her soul has entered the iron—this is what Bennett must do if his discussion in *The Author's Craft* is to be more than a glib rationalization of a mind preoccupied with the facts of life, and in order to give the lie conclusively to both Virginia Woolf's and Henry James's view of his art.

It is in *Clayhanger* that Bennett most effectively portrays the interconnectedness of external and internal worlds, and he does so in large part through his symbolism. The novel concerns the young manhood of Edwin Clayhanger, from the time he leaves school to enter his father's business in the Five Towns to the time he obtains the woman he will marry; it shows him from the time of his domination by his father, thwarted in his artistic and sexual desires, to the time of his triumph over his father, dominating his father's household and conquering the woman his father once denied him. This oedipal struggle—or the nexus of love and hate upon which it is based—permeates the world in which Edwin lives; it creates the scenes that he witnesses, the customs of his country, the stances that he takes. What he sees is what he is; what he sees determines in part what he becomes; what he is determines in part what he sees and how he sees it.

Perhaps the central scene in the novel is the celebration of the Sunday School Centennial (a scene which Bennett witnessed as a youth and which, according to a still surviving contemporary from the Five Towns, he describes inaccurately). In this scene Edwin's mind seemingly displays itself in the merely superficial and fragmentary manner of the realistic tradition. He seems to respond to the external world in the most prosaic sense possible. Before the Centennial he is described as scorning it—to everyone except his father—as intellectually beneath him. He possesses a lingering hatred for Sunday School " as a malicious device of parents for willfully harassing and persecuting inoffensive, helpless children." But public opinion and curiosity force him to modify his indifference. He wears his best clothes to the celebration. When the procession begins, " a power not himself drew Edwin to the edge of the pavement." He smells the perspiration of the paraders and immediately is " saddened as by pathos. His attention is interrupted by the appearance of his pregnant sister Clara. He is " self-conscious and awkward " in the formalities of greeting her and reacts against her wry comment on the grandness of his clothes. He knows that had he been wearing a hat, he would not have taken it off to her, although he would have wanted to; he wishes that he and his relatives could conduct themselves with more dignity toward each other. He is also ashamed of her pregnancy: " Other men's sisters, yes; but his! " He thinks she looks ugly and recalls fleetingly her gracefulness as a child. He realizes that she probably looks down upon him for being

unmarried. Her deference in referring to her husband
Albert annoys him, for he thinks that Albert is tedious and
egotistical. Then he is bored by the petty conversation
that ensues and a moment afterward is hurt by her hostile
reference to his developing friendship with the Orgreaves.
But a sudden phrase by her evokes a strong memory and
transforms his feelings: " he could hear again the girl of
fourteen. His heart at once softened to her. The impartial
and unmoved spectator that sat somewhere in Edwin . . .
thought how strange this was."

These are Edwin's initial responses to the scene. They
string themselves out over a few pages. None of them is
elaborated. Little emphasis is laid upon the simultaneity
and contradictoriness of any of them. For the most part
they follow in an orderly procession after fragments of
speech and observation. The remaining pages proceed in
the same fashion, but even on the surface they suggest
more psychological insight than Bennett is usually credited
with. Edwin feels his heart beating when Hilda (the girl
with whom he is falling in love) appears, and he sinks
into a dreamlike state. He finds her physically repulsive
and thinks her boldness toward him is like a physical
wound inflicted upon him. Then he feels " violent against
her " and later thinks to himself, " If I had you to myself,
my lady, I'd soon teach you a thing or two! " At the same
time, " he was undeniably proud to be seen in the streets
with a disdainful, aloof girl." The singing of " Rock of
Ages " at the climax of the ceremony inexplicably reduces
him to tears. " ' Why the deuce do I want to cry? ' he
asked himself angrily and was ashamed." Through the
mist in his eyes he sees an inscription on one of the banners,
" The Blood of the Lamb," and in his mind's eye sees " the
riven trunk of a man dying, and a torrent of blood flowing
therefrom and people like his Auntie Clara and his brother-

in-law Albert plunging ecstatically into the liquid in order to be white." Then while he listens to a hymn, " a phrase from another hymn jumped from somewhere into his mind. . . . The phrase was ' India's coral strand.' " Even as he watches the colorful pageant:

> . . . it seemed to him that he was not in England any longer. It seemed to him that in the dim cellars under the Shambles behind the Town Hall, where he had once been, there dwelt, squatting, a strange and savage god who would blast all those who did not enter his presence dripping with gore, be they child or grandfather. It seemed to him that the drums were tom-toms, and Baines' a bazaar. He could fit every detail of the scene to harmonize with a vision of India's coral strand.

The mist before his eyes clears, and he sees his father across the way at the window of the bank. He turns and says derisively to an uncomprehending Hilda, " ' More blood! . . . It only wants the Ganges at the bottom of the Square—! . . .' he wished to trample on her feelings. She roused the brute in him, and perhaps no-one was more astonished than himself to witness the brute stirring." A few minutes later his and Hilda's attention to the ceremony is interrupted by the appearance of the old and doddering Sunday School teacher, Shushions, who is beset by a policeman and some young men. Hilda urges Edwin to help him. Edwin at first barely recognizes Shushions, and he feels awkward in going forward: " he loathed public altercations." But examining closely the ruined old man, he is suddenly

> . . . revolted by the spectacle of the younger men baiting him. He was astonished that they were so short-sighted as not to be able to see the image of themselves in the old man, so imprudent as not to think of their own future. . . . He

wanted . . . to protect the old man not only from the insults
of stupid and crass bullies, but from the old man himself,
from his own fatuous senility. He wanted to restore to him
by a benevolent system of pretences the dignity and the
self-respect which he had innocently lost, and so to keep him
decent, to the eye if not to the ear. . . . And it was for his
own sake, for the sake of his own image, as much as for
the sake of the old man, that he wanted to do this.

He makes a gesture to intercede, and Hilda then assists
Shushions:

The transformation in her amazed Edwin, who could see
the tears in her eyes. The tableau of the little silly old man
looking up, and Hilda looking down at him, with her lips
parted in a heavenly invitation . . . was imprinted forever in
an instant, and in an instant dissolved, but for Edwin it
remained one of the epochal things of his experience.

When the ceremony is over and Hilda has left him, Edwin
thinks only that "this is a funny way of spending a
morning."

Isolated from one another as many of Edwin's thoughts
and feelings seem to be by the circumstances that call them
forth, they nevertheless reveal certain consistencies and coherence. They show him to be a somewhat unstable, in-
decisive, shy, sensitive, and imaginative young man. His
attitudes toward Hilda and his sister Clara parallel each
other: his sense of their ugliness, his sense of the indecency
of the one and the boldness of the other, his thought that
they both feel superior, his sudden transforming visions
of them. In a somewhat different way his feelings toward
his father and toward religion intertwine. He does not
ridicule the Centennial to his father beforehand, and he
is affected by the actual spectacle. At the height of his
response to the Centennial, just after he imagines seeing

a dying man's torrent of blood into which his relatives are plunging, he sees his father across the square. Presumably both the ritual and his father are in his mind when he says " More blood " to Hilda.

The crux of the Centennial lies with the two main images that present themselves to Edwin's mind during the scene. One of them is imaginative (although inspired by the real scene) and the other is real (although probably exaggerated in Edwin's mind) : one is of the dying man, the dying cellar god, whose blood from his riven trunk becomes the Ganges river for Edwin's relatives to purify themselves in; the other is of Hilda bending kindly over the old Sunday School teacher, Shushions. The two images are obverse reflections of each other: the central figure of each is a dying or old man of some religious consequence, toward whom hatred (" More blood ") or loving-kindness is expressed. They reflect, dream and reality, the conflict in Edwin's soul with regard to his father.

These two images are central to the novel; they relate to all of the other images of the novel, from the first scene to the last, as Edwin's mind displays itself against the world of the Potteries. In the first scene of the novel Edwin is shown loitering for a moment on a bridge over a canal. He sees a horse on a tow-path drawing a canal boat and behind the horse a little girl belaboring the animal with a whip. " Edwin . . . stared uninterested at the spectacle of the child, the whip, and the skeleton [the horse]." He hardly sees what he looks at: " He had left school that day, and what his eyes saw as he leaned on the bridge was not a willing beast and a gladdened infant [gladdened because she has been given the use of the whip for the first time], but the puzzling world and the advance guard of its problems bearing down on him." On realistic grounds the sight is one that Bennett chooses at random from among

a multitude of possibilities (although Bennett's putative
ancestor, James Brindley, built the actual canal, and Bennett may have been partial to the place) ; likewise on realistic grounds Edwin ignores the sight because he is day-
dreaming. In fact Bennett chooses the sight because it is
peculiarly appropriate, and Edwin in staring at it does not
ignore it but transforms it into his own dilemma. What
Edwin sees in the external world is what he sees in his
internal world: the child beating the old canal horse is
Edwin gaining the whip hand over the old river god, his
father.

When Edwin abandons his reverie and goes home, he
finds his father talking to old Shushions. Shushions can
claim credit for Edwin's very existence, since some forty
years ago he saved Darius's life. In senile pride over his
benefaction he shakes Edwin's hand and drops a tear from
his eye. To Edwin, Shushions means nothing, but the
tear startles him: " the tear was so genuine, so convincing,
so majestic that it induced in Edwin a blank humility."
As a scene of benefaction and tears, this moment is the
first of many similar scenes, prefiguring—for example—the
Sunday School scene in which Shushions is the object of
Hilda's benefaction, and the scene at the end of the novel
in which Edwin bends compassionately over Hilda. Its
significance to Edwin is that it presents him with the basic
contrast to the child beating the helpless old horse; it
presents him with one of the extreme choices he can make.
He will in the end have a father who has been reduced to
an image of Shushions, and he will in the end confront
a woman who because of her cruelty to him " he could
have taken . . . and beaten." In the two contrasting images
as they develop over the course of the novel—sometimes
as real, sometimes as imaginary scenes—lie the basic attitudes toward life made available to Edwin. The elements

of the first image—the child, the old horse, the whip, and the canal—are the primary symbols of his situation.

Book One of the novel concerns the subjection of Edwin's artistic impulses to his father's will. The action involves two similar images, one real and the other metaphorical: Edwin saving the structure of his father's shop and Darius destroying " the . . . structure of his [Edwin's] hopes." Edwin has been working about a week for his father when he prevents a catastrophe in the shop. Darius has bought a secondhand machine, one already " ' broken in,' as it were a horse." The weight of the machine, added to the undue burden to which Darius has long subjected the second-floor shop, threatens to shatter the floor. Edwin " could not kill in his mind the hope that the floor would yield," but then, " hardly knowing what he did, and certainly not knowing why he did it," he prevents disaster by roping the horse-machine to a hook in the ceiling and so removing its weight from the floor. Darius, whose belief in the strength of the floor has been " religious," cries " in the wreck, not of his shop but of his religion." Edwin sees " his father's face working into monstrous angular shapes, and . . . the tears spurt out of his eyes "; he performs the compassionate act; he saves the shop. But he abandons the shop spiritually, abandons his father's " religion "—just as he later rejects the Sunday School Centennial; he gives his father good reason for tears. He wants to become an architect: he will build his own hopes out of the wreckage of his father's wish that he should stay in the shop. In the ensuing conflict Darius's " heavy, obstinate, relentless force . . . was now channelled in one tremendous instinct ": " to save his business." His weight crushes " the whole structure of . . . [Edwin's] hopes." Edwin is defeated: " He could no more change his father than the course of a river." The first phase of his struggle to gain the whip hand, to beat the old river god, ends in defeat.

In Book Two, the struggle shifts its ground somewhat. Edwin's sexual development has received a spur in his watching Florence Simcox's clog dance in Book One. The scene occurs on the same day he enters his father's business, and memories of it recur on psychologically appropriate occasions later in the novel: when he makes his first decision to ask his father to allow him to become an architect, when his relationship with Janet Orgreave first develops in the house Darius is building, when he takes over control of the business from Darius, and at the banquet just before Darius's death. The dance occurs in Book One, but not until Book Two does Edwin involve himself directly with either Janet or Hilda, the girl with whom he falls in love. The struggle shifts from Edwin's architectural desires to his sexual desires as they conflict with the demands of his father and the shop. Nevertheless, an image of the earlier struggle lingers in the shape of the new house that Darius builds. His first serious encounters with both Janet and Hilda occur in this house during its construction. The beginning of the experience with Hilda is important. Edwin has spent an evening with the Orgreaves and has met Hilda for the first time there. He has barely spoken to her. Now he comes over alone in the dark to look at the house, and because he has no key he enters through the cellar.

> He crouched down under the blank east wall, and, feet foremost, disappeared slowly, as though the house were swallowing him. He stood on the sillage of the cellar, and struck a match. Immense and weird, the cellar; and the door-less doorway, leading to the cellar-steps, seemed to lead to affrighting matters. He was in the earth. . . . He trembled, he was afraid, exquisitely afraid, acutely conscious of himself amid the fundamental mysteries of the universe.

It is a few days later that the Sunday School Centennial occurs and with it Edwin's vision of the dying cellar god

of the East. In the cellar of his father's house he dimly
perceives that he has invaded the god's sanctuary (without
a key, without right or power) ; presumably he appreciates
the sexual aspect of his invasion (without a key). He goes
upstairs and sees Hilda coming across the way in the dark
to speak to him.

Over a year passes, during which time Edwin does not see
Hilda, who lives in another town. Then within four days
after they meet again, they plight their troth with a kiss.
Before this moment Edwin walks with Hilda past the
" Blood Tub," Snagg's Theatre, where once " melodrama
and murder and gore " could be seen. Hilda wonders at
such crudity in the Five Towns; but Edwin, who at the
Sunday School Centennial could imagine the torrent of
blood flowing from the god in the shambles, replies, " It's
our form of poetry, I suppose." They go inside and witness
a strike meeting, an act of rebellion against authority; they
see " tigerish passion " and hear " dangerous growls . . . in
running explosions." Then they return to the shop, and
Edwin in a " flood-tide of masculinity " confesses his love.
" The embrace was clumsy, in its instinctive and unskilled
violence. . . ." Feeling himself a man momentarily, Edwin
ventures another test with his father; he tells Darius that
he is thinking of marriage and asks for a raise from the
pittance that Darius pays him. Darius ridicules his desire
and need, and defeats him. " In his father's presence he
never could feel that he was a man." But upon Darius's
final insulting suggestion that Hilda could supply some
money, he vows the revenge that he will have:

> As he stood furious and impotent in the hall, he thought,
> with his imagination quickened by the memory of Mr.
> Shushions: " When you're old, and I've *got* you "—he
> clenched his fists and his teeth—" When I've *got* you and
> you can't help yourself, by God it'll be my turn! "

At the Centennial he had been " revolted by the spectacle of the younger men baiting . . . [Shushions]. He was aston- ished that they were so shortsighted as not to be able to see the image of themselves in the old man. . . ." That image of himself in Shushions does not arise here to produce pity. He learns within an hour or so that Hilda has inexplicably married George Cannon. Book Two ends in sexual defeat.

Book Three, " His Freedom," records Edwin's revenge, achieved when Darius deteriorates into an image of Shu- shions. Darius's decline begins on the evening when he buries Shushions, who has died under apparently extremely cruel circumstances at the very workhouse from which he had once saved Darius. Darius returns home, shocked by his experience and crying; and Edwin, who has spent the evening exulting in Gladstone's defense that day in Parlia- ment of Home Rule for Ireland, begins the assumption of his own home rule. Darius in his swift decline becomes like " a victim in a halter "; he seems to Edwin assisting him up the stairs on one occasion like " an incalculable and mysterious beast."

One day Darius, senile and aged beyond his years, wants money to plant mushrooms in the cellar and wants the young servant Jane, " the desired Bathsheba," to help him. Edwin refuses. The image of the dying cellar god Shushions, succored by Hilda " with her lips parted in a heavenly invitation," had been " imprinted forever on Edwin's mind." He denies the dying god Darius such a moment of felicity in the cellar. Darius once refused him money and a woman; now Edwin refuses them to Darius. In that moment " Edwin grew nearly capable of homicide." Later in his father's final agony, Edwin's conscience summons the shame and compassion he felt for Shushions with Hilda: " Why couldn't we have let him grow his mushrooms if he wanted to? . . . Supposing it *had* been a nuisance, supposing he

had tried to kiss Jane . . . , what then? " But at the same
time he thinks: " I shan't be sorry when this is over."

In Book Four Edwin becomes a man; he assumes his
father's position in the house and he resumes his relationship with the woman his father denied him. When he
comes to Hilda in Brighton, never having heard a word
from her to explain or apologize for her jilting of him
and receiving none now, he thinks she ought to be " on her
knees . . . in tears . . . stammering an appeal for forgive-
ness." He thinks that " he could have taken her and beaten
her . . . , made her scream with the pain that his love would
inflict." Hilda's husband has deserted her, and over the
course of months she and Edwin confess their love again.
At the end of the novel Edwin is indeed in his father's
position, sitting in his father's chair, succoring the woman
who once succored the old god Shushions, seeing her face
transfigured now as it was at the Centennial, seeing her
tears too, and feeling deep compassion:

> Somewhere within himself he smiled as he reflected that he,
> in his father's place, in his father's very chair, was thus
> under the spell of a woman. . . . As soon as she felt his
> touch, she dropped to her knees. . . . He bent over a face
> that was transfigured. . . . Drowning amid the waves of her
> terrible devotion, he was recompensed in the hundredth part
> of a second for all that through her he had suffered or might
> hereafter suffer.

It is not to be supposed that Bennett thought that his
hero possessed an unusually subtle mind. He once con-
templated entitling the novel " A Thoughtful Young Man,"
but decided that the public would miss the irony. What
is subtle is the portrait. Edwin's mind constructs itself
between images of violence and compassion, watching a
child beat a horse and giving its love to a weeping woman.
It is a mind created by its environment, taking into itself

the image of the child beating the horse; it is a mind that creates its environment, making Hilda cry before it gives its love. The sort of environmental determination of character that is usually ascribed to the realistic novelist and that Virginia Woolf thought to be an evasion of character-creating is hardly what Bennett is undertaking here. He puts Edwin in the provinces in the same way that Conrad puts Kurtz in the jungle. He is not pouring forth facts of provincial life pell mell, as James imagined. He is selecting images that determine, reveal, and reflect human mentality.

The mind that Bennett creates is hardly Edwin's own mind. Edwin is his father's son, and the images in which he lives are transformations of the images in which Darius lives. When Darius is a child he witnesses two scenes of violence and compassion, more extreme than those that surround Edwin, terrible enough in their power over Darius so that they help to mold Edwin's mind, even though he is never told of them. As a child of nine Darius has a brief stay at the workhouse, called the Bastile. There he witnesses a child being flogged:

> . . . then a captured tiger, dressed like a boy, with darting fierce eyes, was dragged in by the table. . . . Then the rod was raised and it descended swishing, and the blood began to flow; but far more startling than the blood were the shrill screams of the tiger. . . . Then the screaming grew feebler, then ceased; then the blows ceased, and the unconscious infant (cured of being a tiger) was carried away, leaving a trail of red drops along the floor.

Darius along with the rest of his family is saved from the workhouse by Shushions:

> . . . he was . . . pushed out of the Bastile, and there he saw his pale father and his mother, and his little sister, and another man. And his mother was on her knees in the cold

autumn sunshine, and hysterically clasping the knees of the
man, and weeping, and the man was trying to raise her,
and the man was weeping too. Darius wept. The man was
Mr. Shushions.

These images linger in Darius' mind. They are transmitted
to Edwin through other images. At the end of the novel,
when Edwin forces Hilda to her knees by his hardness of
heart, requiring her to be ashamed before he can be
compassionate, he is remembering a scene that he never
witnessed.

Bennett never witnessed the scene either. He obtained
the facts he wanted from a book called *When I Was a Child*,
written by a pottery worker in mid-Victorian England. His
name was not Gradgrind.

CHAPTER 5

Allegory:
Christian and Materialistic

THE PRICE OF LOVE

ONE OF THE interesting phenomena of our times is the imaginative grasp that religion has maintained upon men who have rejected it intellectually. Perhaps the phenomenon begins with Thomas Huxley's assuming a holier-than-thou attitude toward Bishop Wilberforce; it does not end with T. S. Eliot's tacit acknowledgment that religion is poetry that is no longer believed. Among novelists, Hardy, Conrad, Lawrence, Forster, and Joyce are notable for their preoccupation with religion, notable too for the ambiguity of their preoccupation, so that the critic is wary about offering explanations for the phenomenon in single terms: psychological, esthetic, or philosophical.

Bennett's preoccupation with religion is partly evidenced by his frequent depiction of religious scenes, such as the Centennial in *Clayhanger*, comparable scenes in *Anna of the Five Towns* and *The Pretty Lady*, and the whole of *Judith*; it is also evidenced by the attention he gives to supernaturalism in *The Glimpse* and other novels. The less obvious, and perhaps more important, aspect of his preoccupation consists of the reference of the lives and actions of many of his characters to biblical and other religious stories and situations. Some of these allusions are explicit,

some are not. They range from the clear reference of Carlotta Peel's sobriquet, Magda (in *Sacred and Profane Love*) ,
to Mary Magdalene, to the slight suggestion that Clayhanger (which is not a Five Towns name) means flesh-
crucified and refers to Edwin's Christlike sacrifice of himself to his father. There is a problem in pursuing allusions
of the latter sort: to what extent is the validity of one
doubtful allusion strengthened by linking it to other doubtful allusions? The fact that the old god Darius dies when
the young god Edwin is thirty-three may or may not seem
to contribute to Edwin's Christlike quality. But there is
no question about the fundamental fact that religious
allusions permeate Bennett's novels. Their significance for
him is ultimately non-religious.

Bennett was reared in a household that was at least fairly
religious and in a community that was deeply religious.
One of Bennett's sisters has insisted that the family atmosphere was quite enlightened, that after a certain age the
children attended chapel at their own discretion. Moreover,
the chapel that the family attended was not of an enthusi-
astic bent. However, it is clear that Bennett himself reacted
bitterly against formal religion at an early age and retained
his bitterness throughout his life. In his essay "My Religious Experience" he describes his father's "sudden
capricious command that we children should say our
prayers at our mother's knee":

> There was, for me, something revolting in the sentimentality,
> the storybookishness, of this injunction . . . ! Nobody could
> possibly in the history of the world have been in a mood
> more fatal to prayer than I was in the moments when I
> obeyed the command. . . .

By the time Bennett was seventeen he was an avowed
agnostic, delightedly following Huxley's challenge to Glad-

stone in the pages of the *Nineteenth Century*. One of his brothers recalls their "unholy joy" in reading Huxley. (Edwin Clayhanger in *These Twain* reads Huxley "with enormous gusto.") When Bennett left the Potteries at twenty-one, "one of the leading thoughts in my head was that I should be free of chapels and Sunday Schools and the desolation of Sabbaths." Late in life one of his sabbaths would be desolated. On a Sunday morning in 1926, while he was walking along London streets, he heard congregations singing hymns; he returned home and wrote in his *Journal*, " I . . . hated the thought of my youth."

The hatred was directed against formal religion, against ritual, against blind faith and morals. In other respects, Bennett thought of himself as a Christian. In a *Journal* entry of 1896 he wrote: "Essential characteristic of the really great novelist: a Christ-like, all-embracing compassion." His judgment in 1929 in favor of Dostoevsky over Joyce and Lawrence was on the grounds of Dostoevsky's greater compassion. Two of his best non-fictional works, *The Feast of St. Friend* and *The Religious Interregnum* (which are much superior to the better known pocket philosophies like *The Human Machine*), take a definite stance against formal Christianity but an equally definite stance in favor of Christian values. *The Feast of St. Friend* proposes an agnostic celebration of Christmas, and *The Religious Interregnum* discusses the replacement of Christianity by a creed with similar ethics.

Thus Bennett's preoccupation with religion has a double edge, and it seems impossible to ascribe his preoccupation more to one attitude than to another. What is certain is that in a broad sense he employs his religious allusions in the service of his materialistic philosophy. He sees religion as a purely human activity; its beliefs are to be understood in human terms; its dramas are human dramas. The agony of Christ is a unique experience only in the sense that the movement of evolution precludes its repetition; the agony is a human experience, determined biologically, culturally, and individually, that recurs in another unique form in the Five Towns. At least one of Bennett's heroes, Louis Fores in *The Price of Love*, undergoes that agony.

The Price of Love is, like *The Glimpse*, one of Bennett's minor novels. Bennett's own judgment upon it in the *Journal*, " sound but not brilliant," seems just. Its technique, though, approaches brilliance; and the novel serves more readily than any of the other novels to reveal the religious element in Bennett's writing.

Most critics have been concerned with *The Price of Love* as a realistic tale. Harvey Darton says, " It is a particular, not a universal, book. It is a minute study of five people. . . . He is not recording life, but some lives. . . . His power of observation is as true as ever. . . ." Geoffrey West quotes Darton approvingly. J. B. Simons notes " a typically ' naturalistic ' touch " in it, remarks upon Bennett's portraying " the Five Towns' middle classes with accuracy," and says that " in summary it is the narrative of a girl's love for the gentlemanly but dishonest Louis Fores. . . ." Georges Lafourcade remarks upon the novel's " psychological realism," its " strong local atmosphere," its qualities " of a first class detective novel." Walter Allen passes over it briefly; he acknowledges " some excellent characterization " but is perturbed by its " mechanical, melodramatic plot."

On realistic grounds, the novel is approximately what these critics describe it as being. It begins with a birthday party at which Louis Fores and his cousin Julian Maldon independently steal some money belonging to their great-aunt. The theft is discovered, but Mrs. Maldon is unwilling to press any charge against Louis, whom she believes to be the sole guilty person. She dies within a few days of the theft and leaves her wealth to the two men. Louis at the time is courting Rachel, the maid in Mrs. Maldon's home, and Julian (who is a minor figure in the novel) goes off to Africa. In the second part of the novel, which takes place about six months later, Louis confesses his share of the crime to Rachel, to whom he is now married; he does so after Julian, who has returned from Africa, confesses to the two of them that he has stolen the money. Louis and Rachel quarrel and then—as the novel ends—are reconciled. The novel is melodramatic in a limited sense, mainly through atmosphere rather than through action. It is a detective story in the sense that *Crime and Punishment* is a detective story: Louis commits his crime before the eyes of the reader, and his state of mind after the theft rather than any process of uncovering the crime is Bennett's chief interest.

Viewed realistically, the novel has little to do with religion. Beyond Rachel and Louis's indecision over joining chapel, which offers "salvation in the next world," or church, which offers "salvation in this," there is only the most fragmentary reference to religion: one of the characters carrying a Bible in his hand, etc. The way in is devious.

When Julian Maldon returns to the Five Towns from his sojourn in Africa and confesses to the now married Rachel and Louis his share in the theft from his great-aunt, Rachel's response is sympathetic in the extreme. Excusing his crime, thinking only of his suffering, " she perceived that she herself was the one person in the world capable of understanding Julian, the one person who could look after him, influence him, keep him straight. . . ." Louis is disturbed by her attitude, especially by her concomitant coldness toward him. On the following day two runaway horses hit him as he is riding his bicycle, and in a hysterical state afterward he confesses his own share in the theft. He gains some sympathy because of the accident but—unlike Julian—none because of his confession. It is only after he makes his gesture of leaving Rachel, going to the Five Towns Hotel for a few hours, and after he has somewhat absolved himself of the theft by revealing to Rachel her own responsibility for having burned the money in the fire grate, that he fully regains her love. (Louis hid the money in the grate, and while he was deliberating whether he should return it, Rachel lit the fire and unwittingly destroyed the money.)   Rachel then thinks: "He was the man she wanted; the whole rest of the world was nothing in comparison to him."

It can be said that Louis's unconscious recognition of the quality of Rachel's character (which is predominantly sado-masochistic), and the similar quality of his own, determine his actions following Julian's confession. The accident of the succeeding day is not an accident. When Louis is preparing to ride off on his own bicycle, towing a borrowed one behind, Rachel says, "Isn't it dangerous?" Louis responds, "Are you dangerous?" Later, in describing the accident to Rachel, Louis says, "The first horse simply made straight for me. . . . He wanted me, and he had me." Rachel reflects: "A few seconds sooner, a few seconds later— and naught would have occurred to Louis, but he must needs be at exactly a certain spot at exactly a certain instant. . . ." Then Louis, while at the hotel, puts the blame for the accident on Rachel, echoing his earlier rhetorical question about her being dangerous: since he was going off with the borrowed bicycle with the intention of buying Rachel a new one, "his accident was due solely to his benevolence for her." (While he is there, Rachel is thinking to herself, "I am as strong as a horse.") A waiter at the hotel remarks upon the accident: "Strange it should happen to you, sir. A gentleman who was in here the other day said that in his opinion you were one of the cleverest cyclists in the Five Towns." The most interesting—if most dubious—intimation that the accident is something more than a real accident is that the boy with the horses is a kind of image of Louis and also of Rachel. Louis is riding one bicycle and towing the other, and the boy is riding one horse and leading the other; the bicycle Louis is leading has been referred to on a previous occasion—when Rachel was riding it—as a "wild pony," and it is the horse that the boy is leading which first hits Louis.

Louis responds to the accident hysterically. At first he dismisses his wounds as inconsequential; then he thinks he will die. He confesses his share in the theft: "He had despised Julian . . . ; but in his extremity he had been ready to imitate him." His imitation extends beyond confession. Julian deserts his bachelor quarters in Knype and goes to Hanbridge to live; he joins the Knype Ethical Society. Louis deserts Rachel in Bursley and goes to the Five Towns Hotel, which lies between Knype and Hanbridge; the next day he and Rachel attend church for the first time. When he is at the hotel (which is called a "monastery") Louis talks with the Swiss waiter Krupp, whose name is meant to suggest the German war manufacturer. Krupp is a mysterious figure "whose enigma no Staffordshire man had ever penetrated" and who possesses a manner of speech that seems "to deprive his remarks of any human quality." He makes up his story about the gentleman who called Louis an excellent cyclist, and when pressed to identify the man describes him as "a dark gentleman, with a beard, a little lame." The three elements of his description are distinguishing features of Louis, Julian, and Horrocleave and Batchgrew respectively (the latter two are Louis's employer and Mrs. Maldon's trustee) : Louis has black hair,

Julian grows a beard while in Africa, Horrocleave sprains his ankle at work, and Batchgrew shows himself at one point to seem lame in the arm. Louis tells Krupp nothing, and has told no one else, of his vague plan to leave for America, but explains that he is at the hotel to meet an American businessman. An hour or two passes, and then inexplicably Horrocleave appears on the scene to accuse Louis of fleeing England. Horrocleave has recently discovered Louis's peculations at work. He says, " I hear you're off to America."

> Louis looked through the fretted partition at the fretted figure of Krupp alone in the lounge. And Horrocleave also looked at Krupp. And Krupp looked back with his enigmatic gaze, perhaps scornful, perhaps indifferent, perhaps secretly appreciative—but in any case profoundly foreign and aloof and sinister.

Louis sees himself prevented from escaping, and he returns home to a forgiving and self-accusing Rachel. By the next day he has redeemed himself in Rachel's eyes, and he makes a private settlement with Horrocleave—the two agreeing simply to part company. The book closes with Rachel and Louis leaving Horrocleave to go to church.

Louis's salvation, his escape from ignominy, which is sealed by his presumed appearance at church (where in contrast to chapel one achieves " salvation in this " world) , occurs on Easter Sunday, the day of Christ's resurrection. On Easter Saturday Louis is at the hotel, confronted by the demon-like Krupp; and on Easter Saturday Christ descends into Hell. On the Friday before Good Friday Louis immolates himself under horses' hoofs and becomes hysterical, and on Good Friday Christ accepts his destiny and undergoes his agony. However, the name " Louis Fores " sounds not like " Christ " but—with a slight inversion—like " Lucifer." Moreover, if Louis can be said to be saved on Sunday, it is another thief (one of a pair, like Louis and Julian) to whom Christ on the cross says, " Today shalt thou be with me in paradise." And since Louis earlier betrays himself, he is his own Judas.

Who is Louis? It does some violence to Scripture to say that he is Christ, Lucifer, one of the thieves, and Judas all at once; it does some violence to Bennett to say that the possible allusions are to be taken seriously rather than ironically and humorously. However, Bennett was capable of doing violence to Scripture; and it will prove useful, for the purpose of the present chapter, to explore the similarities rather than the contrasts implicit in the allusions. It may also prove useful to carry the investigation well into the realm of conjecture. Although much of the interpretation may seem questionable, the pervasiveness of religious allusion in the novel will become evident.

Comparisons between Christ and Lucifer, and Christ and Judas, have had a long history. Comparison between Christ and a thief is suggested by Christ's words when he is arrested, " Are ye come out as against a thief . . . ?," by the choice that Pilate gives the people to release either Christ or the thief Barabbas, and by Christ's crucifixion between two thieves. From the psychoanalytical standpoint (notably in comments by Freud and Theodor Reik) , these comparisons have been seen to reflect various elements in the oedipal drama. The blasphemy with which Christ is charged is interpreted as intended rebellion against or theft of the father's omnipotence, the father's masculinity. The punishment of crucifixion represents sexual submission; and insofar as Christ passively accepts the punishment (in the Gospels he predicts his crucifixion and Judas hangs himself) , it is self-imposed, in recognition of the guilt attached to the intention as well as to the act. The several figures in the drama—obedient son, rebel, thief, and betrayer—are representatives of a complex that a single mind sustains. Quite apart from the validity of such an analysis, it reflects basic Freudian assumptions about the nature of human mentality: the primacy of sexuality, the ambivalence of feelings, the processes of conscience. These assumptions themselves, widely accepted though they may be, may seem in another epoch to be little more than characteristics of twentieth-century Western civilization. At any rate, Bennett's studies of love and death in *Riceyman Steps* and *Lord Raingo*, and his depiction of the father-son drama in *Clayhanger*, suggest that he saw human psychology very much as Freud did. His presumed identification of Louis with Christ, Lucifer, a thief, and Judas is to be understood to mean, first, that Louis in his complex of attitudes possesses qualities that are exemplified in Christian legend by different personages and, second, that Louis displays a mentality which—for all the uniqueness of his situation in time and place—is not unlike the mentality of other men in distant times and places.

It is in Part Two of the novel that the most important Christian allusions occur. The action of Part Two covers four days, from Thursday to Sunday, six months after the three days of action of Part One. In this total of seven days, the first three are consecutive, whereas the next four have a lapse of one week in the middle of them. The chronology of these four days of Part Two is as follows.

Chapters 9-11

Thursday, a week before Easter.	Louis and Rachel are seen at home, then bicycle riding. They entertain Batchgrew at dinner. Later they quarrel. Still later Julian comes in and confesses.

Chapter 12

| Friday, the following day, through to early Saturday. | Louis has his accident, thinks he is dying, confesses. Rachel is shown rising the next morning. |

Chapters 13-14

| Saturday morning, continued. | Louis and Rachel continue their quarrel. She goes marketing. |

Chapters 15-18

| Saturday afternoon, following a time lapse of exactly one week. Saturday evening. | Rachel visits Julian. Louis goes to the hotel. Upon returning home, they are reconciled. |

Chapter 19

| Sunday morning, the following day, Easter. | Rachel and Louis are seen at home, then at Horrocleave's, then going to church. |

The time lapse from Saturday to Saturday prevents a parallel to Christ's last days from being exact, but it serves realistic necessities. There would be difficulty in establishing the typically realistic atmosphere—everyday business and domestic activities—were the action to surround Good Friday, a holiday calling for the cessation of normal activities. Secondly, Louis could hardly recover from a seemingly serious accident on Good Friday to leave for the Five Towns Hotel the next day and go to Horrocleave's and then to church the following. Most important, for Bennett to make his parallel exact would be to risk losing focus upon his immediate subject: his reader might become as conscious of Christ as of Louis. Bennett keeps his allusions more discreet and less precise than, say, Conrad with his Heyst-Christ parallels in *Victory.*

At the same time, Bennett does his best to close the gap between the two Saturdays, to make them seem one: first, by immediately resuming the action from the first Saturday morning to the second Saturday afternoon (he straddles the gap in a single sentence opening Chapter Fifteen) and, second, by making the actions of the second Saturday afternoon a fulfillment of actions planned for the first Saturday, Rachel having intended to see Julian then and Louis having made an even more feeble effort to leave her then. Had these two actions been carried out on the first Saturday, presumably the third action of the day, Louis and Rachel's reconciliation, would have been also. The four days of Part Two are to all intents and purposes consecutive; they are the four days from Holy Thursday to Easter Sunday.

On Thursday Louis is shown in two scenes that prefigure his accident; both suggest elements of Christ's crucifixion. The first occurs with his and Rachel's hanging of Leighton's "The Garden of the Hesperides" in the bedroom. The Greek legend of the golden apples is similar to the story of Adam and Eve, which is the first cause of Christ's crucifixion.

> Then Louis raised himself on his toes and raised his left arm with the nail as high as he could and stuck the point of the nail against a pencil-mark on the wall. Then he raised the right hand with the hammer. . . .

If Louis's accident and Christ's crucifixion can be regarded as self-immolations, the image is an appropriate prefiguration. In the ensuing conversation with Rachel, Louis suggests that he hit her finger with the hammer. Rachel "would have taken pleasure in the pain." So Mary suffers at Christ's crucifixion: " Yea, a sword shall pierce through thy own soul also." The second scene is the bicycle lesson a few minutes later. On this occasion it is Rachel who has the accident. Louis maliciously pushes her off to ride alone; and inexperienced as she is, she falls. She is not hurt but sits up " full of secret dolors." Then she falls again, frightened by an approaching tram-car. (When Louis has his accident, she asks him, " But was it the tram-car you ran into? ") Again, " hard knocks had not hurt her." But envious of Louis's ability to ride, she had said to him earlier, " I can't bear to see you ride so well. . . . I should like to hurt you frightfully." Mary in her dolor becomes Christ-like: the sword that pierces her soul is like the lance that pierces his side at the crucifixion. Rachel is most obviously like Louis in her middle name, which is Louise, the name that Louis calls her in moments of intimacy. When Louis does have his accident, his side bears seven bruises, suggestive of Mary's seven dolors.

In the action of the rest of the evening—Rachel and Louis entertaining Batchgrew at dinner, then quarrelling, and later receiving Julian and hearing his confession—there is material that may call to mind Christ's betrayal that occurs on Thursday. Louis and Batchgrew discuss the investment of Louis's inheritance, and Batchgrew points out a scheme under which Louis would receive thirty to thirty-five shillings for every pound invested. That the sum is meant to suggest the thirty pieces of silver for which Judas betrays Christ is perhaps indicated by references elsewhere to comparable figures. Louis when he adjusts Horrocleave's petty-cash book " had been prepared for a deficit of twenty-five, or even thirty " pounds and is staggered to discover he has stolen seventy-three, which sum means that " in addition to his salary, some thirty shillings a week had been mysteriously trickling through the incurable hole in his pocket "; toward the end of the book, when he deserts Rachel, he has "about thirty pounds" with him.

A little later in the evening, after Batchgrew has gone, a shabby messenger boy arrives with a note from Julian, who wants to call. Louis, who in the eyes of his servant has just appeared to be a "superior being," comes into the parlor:

> Louis, elegant, self-possessed, and superior, passed into the parlor exactly as if the messenger had been invisible. He was separated from the messenger by an immeasurable social prestige. He was raised to such an altitude above the messenger that he positively could not see the messenger with the naked eye. And yet for one fraction of a second he had the illusion of being so intimately akin to the messenger that a mere nothing might have pushed him into those vile clothes and endowed him with that furtive look and that sinister aspect of a helot. For one infinitesimal instant he was the messenger and shuddered.

Like the boy on the horse, like Krupp at the hotel, like Rachel, like some of the other characters, the messenger boy is an image of Louis himself. Several aspects of the earlier description of him—mainly his delicate features and graceful carriage—strengthen the comparison. He is, in Christian terms, Christ the man, the same as and yet immeasurably distant from Christ the god; he is the man in whom Christ shudders in his agony. His function is to announce the betrayal, the self-betrayal, that occurs or recurs with the confession that Julian comes to make.

Julian has presumably been in Africa for six months and his appearance in the Five Towns is until this moment unknown to Rachel and Louis, although it is suspected by them. When he enters, his countenance seems to say, "You've wanted me to come, and I've come." Louis has good reason to fear Julian, whose share in the theft is not known; he awaits Julian's words in fear that Julian may accuse him of the entire theft. When Julian does confess, " He confessed as one who accuses." In the respect that his confession and Rachel's response to it put an unbearable burden upon Louis that Louis tries to discharge through his accident and his own subsequent confession, it is indeed an accusation. After Louis does confess he realises that although " he had despised Julian . . . , in his extremity he had been ready to imitate him." On Thursday night, too, Judas the thief comes to point the finger at Christ the thief. (" Are ye come out as against a thief . . . ? ")

Louis's accident on the next day has already been discussed as his crucifixion. Some additional elements of it have Christian overtones. In the account of Christ's crucifixion in the Gospel of St. Mark occur the following passages.

> And they gave him to drink wine mingled with myrrh: but he received it not.

> And one ran and filled a sponge full of vinegar, and put it on a reed, and gave him to drink. . . .

Louis in describing his accident to Rachel says:

> First thing I knew I was the center of an admiring audience and fat Mrs. Heath, in her white apron and steel hanging by her side, was washing my face with a sponge and a basin of water, and Heath stood by with brandy.

It is soldiers who press the wine upon Christ and sponge his face. Heath in *The Price of Love* is a butcher; the long steels that hang at his and his wife's sides are swordlike; Heath himself is described at one point as possessing a " salute somewhat military in gesture." Subsequently Christ's body is wrapped in linen and then buried. Louis is wrapped in linen bandages by Mrs. Heath. A week later, on Saturday, when he goes to the Five Towns Hotel, he purchases a linen suit for his projected trip to America.

In the several hours following Louis's accident, his words and behavior with Rachel can perhaps be said to suggest the seven last words of Christ. Three of the possible parallels are worth mentioning. Christ's " My God, my God, why hast thou forsaken me? " may be echoed in " Well, what price me as a victim of the Inquisition! " Upon the words " I thirst," soldiers offer Christ vinegar, which he takes (in St. Mark he is offered wine with myrrh but rejects it) ; and twice Rachel forces Louis to drink against his will. Lastly Christ cries, " It is finished."

> Now from the sixth hour there was darkness over all the land unto the ninth hour.
>
> And about the ninth hour Jesus cried. . . .
>
> Jesus when he had cried again with a loud voice, yielded up the ghost.
>
> And, behold, the veil of the temple was rent in twain . . . and the earth did quake, and the rocks rent.

Note the three-hour lapse in time, the suggestion of death in Christ's words, and the storm. In *The Price of Love* the comparable passage reads:

> And when, about three hours later, he murmured, " Old girl, I feel pretty bad. . . ."
>
> " I knew it," she said to herself.
>
> His complaint was like a sudden thunderclap in her ears, after long faint rumblings of a storm.

Louis, like Christ, revives—or survives; the Staffordshire *Signal* calls the accident a " Providential Escape." At first Louis dismisses his injuries lightly, whereas Rachel thinks he is dying. The doctor assures Rachel that the injuries are not serious and tells her not to believe Louis if he says that he is dying. Later Louis does believe he is dying, confesses his sins, and reproaches Rachel for not responding sympathetically: "You don't seem to understand that I'm dying." Rachel now "knew that he was not dying, that he was in no danger whatever . . . ," and she condemns his crime and his character: "The vilest quality in him was his capacity to seem innocent." Louis on the next morning, "delivered from the appalling fear of death," thinks about his crime: "For the sake of placating Omnipotence let it be deemed a theft. . . . He knew that with all of his sins he . . . [was] a model for mankind."

Artistically, the most impressive Christian allusion occurs in a scene very early Saturday morning. The relevant passage from the Gospels is the description in Matthew of events following the crucifixion:

> And the graves were opened; and many bodies of the saints which slept arose,

> And came out of the graves after his resurrection, and went into the holy city. . . .

In the scene in the novel, Rachel rises at about five A. M., convinced that Louis will not die. She draws the blinds, opens the window, and looks out upon a rain-washed neighborhood. Then she sees a strange sight.

> A man came hurrying with a pole out of the western vista of the lane, and stopped in front of the gas-lamp, and in an instant the flame was reduced to a little fat worm of blue, and the man passed swiftly up the lane, looking straight ahead with bent shoulders, and was gone. Never before had Rachel actually seen the lamp put out. Never before had she noticed, as she noticed now, that the lamp had a number, an identity—1054. The meek acquiescence of the lamp, and the man's preoccupied haste, seemed to bear some deep significance, which however she could not seize. But the aspect of the man afflicted her, and she did not know why.

Then a number of other figures, in a long spasmodic procession, passed up the lane after the man, and were gone out of sight. Their heavy boots clacked on the pavement. They wore thick dirty grayish-black clothes, and dark kerchiefs round their necks; about thirty of them in all, colliers on their way to one of the pits on the Moorthorne ridge. They walked quickly, but they did not hurry as their forerunner hurried. Several of them smoked pipes. . . . Rachel had never seen these pilgrims before, but she had heard them; and Mrs. Maldon had been acquainted with all their footfalls. They were tragic to Rachel; they infected her with the most recondite horror of existence; they left tragedy floating behind them in the lane like an invisible but oppressive cloud.

The lamplighter is like Christ, who lights the world and who puts out the light with his death. The pole he bears upon bent shoulders is like the cross that Christ carries to Calvary. The miners who are pilgrims are going to their graves, the pits, in a reverse image of the saints rising from the graves. The tragedy of their lives is the tragedy of human existence that Christ sacrifices himself to redeem.

There are several other aspects of the religious element in the novel. Batchgrew, for example, is portrayed as one of the scribes and Pharisees. He is a councillor and "a religionist," just as the scribes were teachers of law and the Pharisees a sect notable for adherence to religious rites and the ceremonies of law. He is the same hypocrite that they were. A comparison of passages from the novel with passages from Matthew suggests other similarities:

> For they bind heavy burdens and grievous to be borne, and lay them on men's shoulders. . . .

> Mr. Batchgrew eyed the affrighted creatures with satisfaction, appearing to take a perverse pleasure in thus imposing upon them the horrid incubus.

· · · ·

And love the uppermost rooms at feasts. . . .

He ate the supper; he kept on eating it; he passed his plate with alacrity; he refused naught.

                    .   .   .

And [love] greetings in the markets. . . .

She [Rachel] had never been into the Covered Market [before] because Mrs. Maldon had a prejudice against its wares. . . . She passed a secondhand bookstall without seeing it . . . it was made visible to her by the fact that Councillor Thomas Batchgrew was just emerging from the shop behind it, with a large volume in his black-gloved hands [an old Bible, printed in Bursley]. Thomas Batchgrew came out of the dark book-shop as a famous old actor, accustomed to decades of crude public worship, comes out of a fashionable restaurant into a fashionable thoroughfare. His satisfied and self-conscious countenance showed that he knew that nearly everybody in sight was or ought to be acquainted with his identity and his renown. . . .

                    .   .   .

. . . for ye devour widows' houses. . . .

For when he supervened into an environment [Batchgrew has just entered the widow Maldon's house for the first time in the novel] he had always the air of an animal on a voyage of profitable discovery. [Batchgrew, who is Mrs. Maldon's trustee, does not devour her house while she is alive—purely from discretion. He seems to Rachel, after Mrs. Maldon's wealth has passed to the grandnephews, to have " safeguarded Louis's interest under the will in order to rob him afterwards. . . ."]

One of the habits or rites of Pharisees is the frequent washing of their hands. In this respect most of the characters in the novel can be considered pharisaical. Finical Mrs. Maldon keeps her house " clean . . . almost in the Dutch sense " despite the dust-laden atmosphere from the potbanks. Rachel, who is at one point called " pharisaical,"

is to Mrs. Maldon " a treasure beyond pearls " because she
shares Mrs. Maldon's sense of cleanliness. When she washes
silverware she is engaged in an " impressive rite." Batchgrew characteristically wears gloves and is shown at one
point taking them " finickingly from the white slop basin
as though fishing them out of a puddle." Louis washes his
hands after adjusting Horrocleave's petty-cash book. Julian
washes his hands just prior to stealing Mrs. Maldon's money.
Mrs. Tams, the servant, performs " the religious . . . rite "
of washing the porch.

There are in the novel several other images, visual and
metaphorical, some of them repeated many times, that have
religious overtones. Apart from their function in this respect, they serve more broadly, along with some other
imagery, to give the novel an impressive coherence. The
incandescent lamp that hangs in the sitting room suggests
an ornate sanctuary lamp that hangs out of reach above
an altar:

> If the tap had been half an inch higher or herself half an
> inch shorter, she [Rachel] would have had to stand on a
> chair instead of a footstool. . . . But heaven had watched
> over this detail. The gas-fitting consisted of a flexible pipe,
> resembling a thick black cord, and swinging at the end of it
> a specimen of that wonderful and blessed contrivance, the
> inverted incandescent mantle, within a porcelain globe. . . .

Rachel's mounting the footstool to tend the lamp suggests
an act at an altar, as does her act later in the kitchen with
Louis:

> Suddenly Rachel tore a strip off the newspaper, folded the
> strip into a spill, and lighting it at the gas, tendered it to
> Louis' unlit cigarette. . . . The gesture with which she
> modestly offered the spill was angelic; it was divine; it was
> one of those phenomena which persist in a man's memory

for decades. At the very instant of its happening he knew
that he should never forget it.

(Louis's feelings resemble Edwin's in *Clayhanger* when
Hilda assists Shushions at the Sunday School Centennial.)
Elements of these images recur in succeeding images.
On the next day Mrs. Maldon tries to recall to Batchgrew
where she put the two sets of banknotes; she says, " I didn't
turn the gas up. I pushed a chair up to the cupboard with
my knee, for me to stand on. I'm certain I put some of
the notes on the top of the cupboard." It is not long after
she has put some of the notes there that Julian sees that
a picture on the cupboard wall " was hung very crooked,"
and in standing on a chair to set it straight discovers the
notes and steals them. Months later when he confesses his
crime, he puts an equal sum back in the same spot when
Rachel and Louis refuse to accept it from his hands. Some
time after Louis hears Mrs. Maldon reconstruct what she
did with the money, he himself goes to the cupboard. In
Part Two Louis and Rachel hang their picture in the bedroom. She stands on a chair to help. Louis intends to
hang a picture done by Mrs. Maldon's son, a picture that
" for thirty years had been an altar for undying affection."
Upon Rachel's protest he hangs instead " The Garden of
the Hesperides " and—like Julian—" flicked it into exact
perpendicularity." (Both the Greek and the Christian
legend of the apples concern theft of a sort.)

A multitude of other images relate to these. Mention
should be made of one—a series itself—that begins with
Louis dropping his share of the money into the fire grate
that is lighted subsequently by Rachel. The image recurs
most notably with Julian's written confession being thrust
by Rachel into the fire. When Louis so loses his money he
absolves himself of his crime, and when Rachel learns that
she was the one to start the fire she thereupon absolves

him. Similarly when she thrusts Julian's confession into
the fire she means to absolve him. Before the altars in
this house, thefts are committed and absolution is won.
When Jesus casts the money changers out of the temple,
he says to them, " My house shall be called the house of
prayer; but ye have made it a den of thieves."

The general significance of the religious allusions in the
novel has been stated in psychological terms. It can be
stated in other terms. Consider one more scene with religious overtones. Just before Rachel and Louis visit the
butcher shop in Part One, they go into Ted Malkin's
grocery store. Rachel has had pricks of conscience about
being seen with Louis while Mrs. Maldon lies ill. She
ignores them: " the voice within her was hushed." But as
she enters the shop, " the voice renewed its monotonous
phrase, and she blushed. The swift change took her by
surprise and frightened her. She was not in Bursley, but
in some forbidden city without a name, pursuing some
adventure at once shameful and delicious." One of the
sustained images of the novel (repeated more than a hundred times) depicts Rachel and Mrs. Maldon as " women
in a city about to be sacked," and—considering the Christian allusions—it might be supposed that Bennett is thinking of Jerusalem, which was sacked in 70 A. D. But the term
" forbidden city " suggests Peiping or Lhasa. Furthermore,
Rachel is in quest of Singapore pineapple. Most likely,
the city is not a city but the Garden of Eden, at whose
gates were set cherubim and a sword to prevent reentry
when Adam and Eve were cast out. " Forbidden " applies
to the " shameful " apple (the pineapple) that Rachel is
pursuing; the " delicious " adventure is the pursuit of
" Singapore Delicious Chunks." Rachel is Eve in the
Garden of Eden; the inward voice that she hushes is " the
voice of the Lord God walking in the garden." The pine-

apple is an apple of great price: Rachel chooses to buy
it in Malkin's shop at 8½d. rather than in another shop
at 7½d. To Malkin Rachel's buying his pineapple is a
" heavenly incident "; to his virgin aunt it is something
else:

> As Rachel, followed by Louis Fores, crossed the shop, Miss
> Malkin looked at them and closed her lips, and lowered her
> eyelids, and the upper part of her body seemed to curve
> slightly, with the sinuosity of a serpent. . . .

(A strange serpent, surely.) When Rachel emerges from
the shop " she had the illusion of being . . . in the midst of
a terrific adventure the end of which none could forsee,"
presumably the human adventure that has followed the
fall. A few minutes later the butcher, like a censorious god
or devil who has witnessed the fall, asks Louis out of the
clear sky, " You're not married, are ye, sir? "

The point is that Louis and Rachel can be compared not
only to Christ and Mary but also to Adam and Eve. They
are players in a recurring drama that concerns love and
death, the preservation of the race, evolution. In the final
chapter of Part One of the novel, entitled " End and Beginning," Mrs. Maldon who lies dying, and Mrs. Tams, who
is tending her, think of Louis and Rachel:

> In the heart of the aged woman exanimate on the bed,
> and in the heart of the ageing woman whose stout, coarse
> arm was still raised to the gas-tap, were the same sentiments
> of wonder, envy, and pity, aroused by the enigmatic actions
> of a younger generation going its perilous, instinctive ways
> to keep the race alive.

In the closing lines of Part One, the lovers learn that Mrs.
Maldon is dying:

> Louis and Rachel glanced at each other, scared, shamed,

even horrified, to discover that the vast pendulum of the
universe was still solemnly ticking through their ecstasy.

As a dominant theme of the novel, evolution is dealt with
in many ways. Much of the material is couched in religious
terms. Mrs. Maldon is described as a goddess who by the
" enchantment " of her facial expression " created goodness
and good will—even out of their opposites "; she is " the
fount of good things "; her house is " invisibly protected."
The course of the novel describes her dethronement and the
establishment of a new goddess. In Part Two, when Rachel
becomes mistress, what was once " dogma was exploded ";
now Rachel becomes " the omniscient, the all-powerful, the
giver of good."

The religious symbolism in *The Price of Love* is possibly
more pervasive than it is in any of Bennett's other novels
except *The Pretty Lady*. But an examination of other works
will bring to light considerable religious allusion. Even in
The Old Wives' Tale, which seemingly is notable for a
sparcity of such allusions, there may be found several scenes
with religious overtones. One of them prefigures Rachel's
visit to Malkin's shop in search of pineapple. The Garden
of Eden in *The Old Wives' Tale* has an obvious name:
Sylvain's Restaurant. Here, along with cocottes pursuing
their trade, Sophia and Gerald take supper. On a table
before them are many fruits; Sophia asks Gerald to order
her a pineapple. The conversation shortly thereafter turns
upon the guillotining that is to take place in two days.
The intended victim had killed a celebrated prostitute who
had " made a lot of money, and retired to her native town."
Not yet a woman of the world, Sophia blushes at the story.

> Sophia felt mysteriously uncomfortable, disturbed by sinister,
> flitting phantoms of ideas which she only dimly apprehended.
> Her eyes fell. Gerald laughed self-consciously.

It would appear that the scales of the snake are upon Gerald Scales. But Sophia does not succumb as Eve and Rachel do. "She would not eat any more pineapple."

Another scene in *The Old Wives' Tale* is a comical version of Louis's crucifixion in *The Price of Love*. In the spring of the year, Dick Povey, the only son of Daniel Povey, cousin of Samuel, learns to ride a boneshaker, a primitive sort of bicycle. He achieves success in a ride that at perilous speed takes him down King Street "straight for the church, as though he meant to disestablish it and perish." He is picked up from "a green grave" inside the churchyard by his father. "His first words were: 'Dad, did you pick my cap up?' The symbolism of the amazing ride did not escape the Square. . . ." The symbolism, indeed, seems obvious.

Dick Povey gives place to another image of Christ, Cyril Povey. On this same occasion the cousins Povey become friends. Daniel is a capable and upright man yet at the same time "a worshipper of the god Pan." In a few succeeding weeks he teaches Samuel "Pan's most intimate lore." The next thing Samuel knows is that Constance is pregnant—she who in over six years of married life has not borne a child. On Sunday Samuel goes to Axe to tell Mrs. Baines, and when he returns "a wind from Arabia wandering cooled his face." He is overwhelmed: "What! A boneshaker, his cousin, and then this!" The events seem to be related—perhaps they are unspeakably related, as Bennett said in his letter to his friend. In Frazer's *The Golden Bough* occurs the following discussion of the cult of Pan in Greece.

> The representative of the god was annually slain for the purpose . . . of maintaining the divine life in perpetual vigor, untainted by the weakness of age; and before he was put to death it was not unnatural to stimulate his reproductive powers in order that these might be transmitted in full activity to his successor. . . .

Daniel is put to death some years later. In her letter to
Sophia many years afterwards, Constance writes, " Cyril
was born . . . at Christmas." The name Cyril means lordly.
On one occasion Constance refers to Cyril as " his lordship."
   One might almost think that Samuel, like Mary's Joseph
or God, is not the father; he needs Daniel's assistance; and
he becomes " a self-conscious parent . . . rather apt to stand
off and pretend that he had nothing to do with the affair ";
and Cyril as a young boy possesses " scarcely any obvious
resemblance to his father." Even earlier Cyril has rejected
his father:

> The baby did not guess that a high invisible god named
> Samuel Povey, whom nothing escaped, and who could do
> everything at once, was controlling his universe from an
> inconceivable distance. On the contrary, the baby was crying
> to himself, There is no God.

   In *Clayhanger* there is an interesting religious allusion
connected with Darius Clayhanger's name. Darius I, king
of Persia, and his successors held their court at Shushan,
capital of the province of Susiana (or Elam); Darius's power
extended into India; the finest pottery of the time and
region is represented by red clay vases. Biblical references
to Shushan occur in the Book of Esther, in which a king
at Shushan decrees the slaughter of Jews, upon which " the
city Shushan was perplexed." In *Clayhanger* the city Shushan is personified by Shushions the Sunday School teacher,
who " by his immense mysterious power, found a superb
situation for Darius "; at the Centennial many years later—
a ceremony described by Edwin as a slaughter of the par-
ticipating children—he is shown as a perplexed old man.
The veins in his face are " Indian Red." Edwin says
caustically of the ceremony, " It only wants the Ganges at
the bottom of the Square—! " He thinks that the crowd is
" under the empire " of religion.

The *Clayhanger* allusion gives some indication of how deeply buried Bennett's religious references can be. It is, at the same time, less doubtful than some of the other allusions that have been suggested. The seemingly slightest, least credible aspect of it, the reference to Indian Red, is possibly the most consciously intended. Bennett could have learned about Indian Red as a pigment when he studied painting in Paris in his maturity; he more likely learned about it as a pottery color in his youth in the Potteries, where for a time he studied art at the Wedgewood Institute, which housed a fine pottery museum. There is reason, then, to suppose that many of his allusions will escape detection, that there are—for example—many more allusions in *The Old Wives' Tale* than a fairly close inspection has revealed. One index of their pervasiveness in his other works is the titles for several of them: *Whom God Hath Joined, These Twain, Sacred and Profane Love, The Old Adam* (the American title for *The Regent*), and *The Gates of Wrath* (which refers to a sacred book of the East). A more interesting index is the names of many of his characters. The one comment that is usually made upon Bennett's names is that he uses his mother's family name of Vernon for the upper level of Five Towns Society. The only other significant comment, by Walter Allen, is that the names of the characters in *Riceyman Steps* are very strange ones—Earlforward, Arb, Raste, Sprickett—names not to be found in the London directory. Many other Bennett names will not be found there. One runs a risk in trying to interpret names, and a few of the suggestions below seem doubtful; however, it is probable that most of Bennett's names possess significance, not necessarily religious. In *Sacred and Profane Love* Diaz suggests Diabolus; during his seduction of Carlotta, Diaz speaks of *Die Götterdämmerung*; his sobriquet for Carlotta is Magda, without question meant to imply Mary Magdalene. In *The Glimpse*, Loring's wife's real name is not Inez but Iris, the name of the Greek goddess of the rainbow; the name is significant most obviously with regard to Loring's perception of persons and things about him as a multicolored "translucent, prismatic sea." Edwin Clayhanger's name has already been discussed. His boyhood friend and alter ego, Charlie Orgreave, bears two Christian nicknames: " The Sunday," and " Old-perish-in-the-attempt." The latter Edwin adopts as his own toward the end of the book. (The nickname was originally Bennett's in his youth.) Hilda Lessway's name suggests the lesser way: " time . . . stood still in the heavens while Hilda sought the way of life "—as against, presumably, the way of the cross. Christine's name in *The Pretty Lady* is obviously Christian. In her sobriquet, the " pretty lady " of the title, is suggested *la belle dame* not so much of Keats and the Middle French poet Alain Chartier as of Christian legend, *la dame avec merci*, the Virgin, whose pity Christine emulates. Earlforward in *Riceyman Steps*, who bears some resemblance to John the Baptist, may possibly in his name suggest the precursor (forward) to the lord (earl) .

Of special interest is the name Henry that Bennett gives to several of his characters: Henry Mynors (" Call me Harry ") of *Anna of the Five Towns*; Denry (a contraction of Edward Henry) Machin of *The Card* and *The Regent*; Henry Earlforward of *Riceyman Steps*; Henry Fausting of the unpublished play *The Return Journey*; and Henry Savott of *Imperial Palace*. Fausting's name in *The Return Journey* is meant to recall Heinrich Faust, a man who was in league with the devil (who himself is familiarly known as " Old Harry ") . Bennett's several characters are somewhat devilish: Henry Mynors, suave and upright, who marries Anna for her money; Denry, an imp if ever a man was; Earlforward, a diabolical miser; and Savott, whose moral arguments justify his reaping where he has not sown. Other names more obviously suggestive of the devil are Diaz, Louis Fores, and T. Racksole (rack soul), the American millionaire of *The Grand Babylon Hotel*. Two other related names are Krupp of *The Price of Love*, and Cannon. In *Hilda Lessways* George Cannon is a petty criminal who ends in jail; in *The Roll-Call* the younger George Cannon goes off to war in the final chapters of the book.

It is worth noting that some of Bennett's surnames for his Five Towns characters are not to be found in the Potteries region. Thomas R. Roberts, who lived in Burslem from 1905 to 1943 and who has done extensive research on Bennett and on Staffordshire history, says that Clayhanger, Fores, Fuge, Horrocleave, Lessways, Scales, and Shushions are unknown to him as surnames and they do not appear in any directories he has consulted. According to Roberts, Clayhanger does appear as a place-name in South Staffordshire and Scales is used elsewhere in England as a place name and is probably used as a surname.

Bennett's religious allusions do not always seem meaningful. The transformation of the city Shushans into Shushions hardly justifies itself in the way that Christ's transfiguration into Louis Fores does. It is possible that many of Bennett's allusions are unconscious, accidental, or merely whimsical. It is also possible that those which seem without purpose have not been carefully enough explored. What is clear is that such allusions permeate the novels, and that in the main they serve Bennett's philosophical outlook. In *The Author's Craft* he writes of the inscrutable reality behind appearances:

> No novelist has yet, or ever will, come within a hundred million miles of life itself. It is impossible for us to see how far we still are from life. The defects of a new con-

vention disclose themselves late in its career. The notion that "naturalists" have at last lighted on a final formula which ensures truth to life is ridiculous. "Naturalist" is merely an epithet expressing self-satisfaction.

In his novels Bennett recapitulates religious allegories and creates his own, trying to come within a million miles of reality. As he said to Henry James, " I know nothing of the middle class."

CHAPTER 6

To Discover Beauty

THE PRETTY LADY

ONE OF THE characteristic critical judgments about Bennett's art is that it is objective, photographic. Two of his critics remark that the use of the auctorial first person at the end of Chapter Five of Book Two of *The Old Wives' Tale* (there is another instance in Chapter Seven of Book One) disfigures momentarily the novel's objectivity. The lapses are unfortunate (as are the similar lapses in *Pride and Prejudice*), but they are not lapses from photographic objectivity. When at the outset of the novel, speaking of fashions in dress in 1862, Bennett says, " Constance and Sophia had the disadvantage of living in the middle ages. The crinoline had not quite reached its full circumference . . . ," he speaks in his own person and speaks in an unmistakable tone. That gravely humorous, gravely ironic tone pervades the novel and is a powerful source of its individual quality.

Some of the more complex ways in which the novel is not objective have already been discussed. Of course, in certain respects Bennett was more nearly objective than many other writers. He did generally avoid first-person intrusions (although it should be noted that he wrote three of his novels in the first person), and he refused to take sides for and against his characters in the Victorian manner and in the contemporary manner of Galsworthy. In the most important respects, though, he regarded his art as personal.

In fact, he saw his art in romantic, explicitly Wordsworthian terms. " All literature," he says in *Literary Taste*, " is the expression of feeling, of passion, of emotion, caused by a sensation of the interestingness of life. . . . The book is nothing but the man trying to talk to you, trying to impart to you some of his feelings." Compare these assertions with Wordsworth's in the Preface to the second edition of *Lyrical Ballads*: poetry is " the overflow of powerful feelings," and the poet is " a man speaking to men." Or compare Bennett and Wordsworth on style:

> [A young writer should] . . . write down, accurately and lucidly and honestly, what he means, always trying to avoid positive ugliness, but not consciously aiming after positive beauty. Let him lose himself completely in the effort to express his meaning in the fewest and clearest words. Good style—beauty, charm, gaiety, splendour, stateliness—will come of itself, unasked and unperceived, so far as the natural distinction of his individuality permits.
>
> *How to Become an Author*

> There will also be found in these volumes little of what is usually called poetic diction; . . . if the poet's subject be judiciously chosen, it will naturally, and upon fit occasion, lead him to passions the language of which, if selected truly and judiciously, must necessarily be dignified and variegated, and alive with metaphors and figures.
>
> *Lyrical Ballads*

These similarities are not accidental. Bennett's discussion of poetry in *Literary Taste* mainly revolves around Wordsworth's poetry and criticism. He says to the reader, " I feel I cannot too strongly press Wordsworth's criticism upon you." From his early years to his last, Bennett displays great admiration for Wordsworth. His novel *Accident*, written in 1926-27, makes considerable thematic use of *The Prelude*.

One should not ignore the realistic aims that were part
and parcel of both Bennett's and Wordsworth's viewpoints
on style as well as on other matters. One should not forget,
either, that Bennett's regional middle class is comparable
to Wordsworth's "humble and rustic life"; that just as
Bennett speaks of "seeing life," so Wordsworth says, "I
have at all times endeavored to look steadily at my subject."
But for Bennett as for Wordsworth the romantic element
in seeing life is inevitable and indispensable. In *The
Author's Craft* Bennett writes: "The novelist is he who,
having seen life, and being so excited by it that he absolutely
must transmit the vision [note the subjective term] to others,
chooses narrative fiction as the liveliest vehicle for the relief
of his feelings." Yet most of Bennett's critics have inferred
no excitement; their typical image of him as a businessman
of letters presupposes the utmost tranquillity in his recol-
lections.

The phrase of Bennett's that most succinctly expresses
his aim as an observant, responsive artist is "to discover
beauty." A slight variation on the phrase occurs in an early
Journal passage, written when he had completed only the
first of his serious novels:

> The day of my enthusiasm for "realism," for "naturalism,"
> has passed. I can perceive that a modern work of fiction
> dealing with modern life may ignore realism and yet be
> great. To find beauty, which is always hidden—that is the
> aim. If beauty is found, then superficial facts are of small
> importance. . . . My desire is to depict the deeper beauty
> while abiding by the envelope of facts. At the worst, the
> facts should not be ignored. They might, for the sake of
> more clearly disclosing the beauty, suffer a certain distor-
> tion. . . .

If it is true—as was argued in Chapter Four—that Bennett
regarded himself as a realist in the most serious sense of

the word, then his aim to find beauty is an intention to penetrate beyond appearances, through the "envelope of facts," to a deeper reality. It is a vision of such a reality, presumably, that he speaks of in *The Author's Craft* as exciting the artist to such an extent that he must transmit it. The individual work of art stems from perception and response; it communicates both vision and feeling.

A few scattered remarks by Bennett repeat and amplify his viewpoint. In his early semi-facetious autobiographical sketch, *The Truth about An Author,* he remarks upon his being "morbidly avaricious of beauty" and looks ahead to all of his future writing as "interminable variations on the theme of beauty." In *Literary Taste,* showing the reader how on occasion a special and intense vision makes an artist of everyone, he says, "Your eyes were unlidded, your ears were unstopped, to some part of the beauty and the strangeness of the world." He puts the same thought in another way later in *The Author's Craft,* affirming that there are two indispensable attributes of a novelist, "the sense of beauty" and a "passionate intensity of vision." What beauty means to him is suggested in an early passage from the *Journal,* in which he describes a visit to the Potteries some eight years after he left them to settle in London:

> . . . when I have been traversing the district after dark, the grim and original beauty of certain aspects of the Potteries . . . has fully revealed itself for the first time. . . . It is not beautiful in detail, but the smoke transforms its ugliness into a beauty transcending the work of architects and of time. Though a very old town, it bears no sign of great age—the eye is never reminded of its romance and history—but instead it thrills and reverberates with the romance of machinery and manufacture, the romance of our fight against nature, of the gradual taming of the earth's secret forces. And surrounding the town on every side are the long straight

smoke and steam wreaths, the dull red flames, and all the
visible evidences of the immense secular struggle for existence. . . .

At about the same time, reviewing George Moore's *A
Mummer's Wife* (the book which opened his eyes to the
beauty of the Potteries) , he writes:

> Mr. Moore in this book ascetically deprived himself of all
> those specious aids to effect—nobility of character, feminine
> grace, the sudden stroke of adverse fate, lovely scenic back-
> ground, splendour of mere event—which the most gifted of
> his forerunners had found useful. . . . And in practising
> such a unique austerity, George Moore produced a master-
> piece. By the singleness of his purpose to be truthful, and
> by sheer power of poetical imagination, he has raised upon
> a sordid and repellent theme an epic tale, beautiful with
> the terrible beauty which hides itself in the ugliness of life.

It is clear from the first of these passages that Bennett
thinks of beauty and romance as virtually synonymous; it
is clear from the second that he sees beauty and truth
similarly. In a letter to Hugh Walpole, written about 1921,
Bennett rejects Walpole's equation of romance and sentimentality; he adds: " It is quite possible to be romantic
and truthful at the same time. All untruthful romance
is vitiated. There is no opposition or mutual excluding
between romance and realism." A comment in *The Arnold
Bennett Calendar* of some years earlier most explicitly unites
beauty (or romance) and truth, and sees them lying both
in the eye of the beholder and in external reality: " The
first and noblest aim of imaginative literature is not either
to tickle or to stab the sensibilities, but to render a coherent
view of life's apparent incoherence, to give shape to the
amorphous, to discover beauty which was hidden, to reveal
essential truth." If Bennett did not consider himself a

spiritual heir to Wordsworth, it must have been because he
felt nearer to John Keats. Keats's dictum, that "what the
imagination seizes as Beauty must be truth," is close to
Bennett's views. At least twice in his writings, Bennett
quotes the last lines of the " Ode on a Grecian Urn " with
complete approval.

Among Bennett's critics, only Walter Allen has discussed
Bennett's preoccupation with beauty, and he seems to have
misconstrued Bennett's customary use of the term. Allen says
that Bennett found beauty " where beauty is lacking " (not
where it is hidden) by creating it through artistic form,
having learned from the French " that beauty lay not in
the matter presented but in the manner in which it was
presented." Bennett paid attention to form (despite being
quite certain that technique is secondary in the production
of the greatest art works), and he gave his novels formal
coherence as a means of capturing beauty. But that he
believed beauty—as he characteristically used the term—to
inhere in manner rather than to be served by it is something
else again. One of his few remarks upon formal beauty
occurs in a passage at the beginning of *Fame and Fiction*,
in which he first asserts, quoting Matthew Arnold to support
him, that matter is of supreme importance in art, and goes
on to remark that the average reader does not understand
beauty of form and that, therefore, " the supreme function
of art, that of creatively interpreting beauty, is rendered
null and inefficacious." Though the passage is not very
clear, Bennett is—in the light of his other comments—distinguishing between formal beauty and beauty which the
artist's shaping mind has discerned in reality. Formal
beauty is essential; the other is more important.

It is apparent that there are ambiguities not only in
Bennett's distinction between two kinds of beauty but also
in his definition of beauty as essential truth. Of particular

importance is his subjective-objective paradox: that an intensity of vision, a shaping vision, is required of the artist and yet that beauty inheres in reality. In his Introduction to Edward Wadworth's *The Black Country*, he recognizes the difficulties that confront him. " I am not such a simpleton," he says, " as to attempt a definition of art," and adds, " assuredly I am not such a simpleton as to attempt a definition of beauty. But I don't mind asserting that beauty is everywhere, and there is naught in which beauty is not." Not being an esthetician, he leaves definition and analysis to others. He asserts what he believes and rests content with his paradoxes. However, he accepts the subjective-objective paradox in a special way that at least moves in the direction of a resolution. For although he can say that " the book is nothing but the man trying to talk to you, trying to impart to you some of his feelings," he is at the same time certain that one sort of feeling is characteristic of the great novelist, a feeling that reaches out from the self to the world in order to know and understand. A *Journal* entry at the outset of Bennett's career reads: " Essential characteristic of the really great novelist: a Christ-like, all-embracing compassion." In an article written in 1910 he says that Dostoevsky's great compassion sets him above almost all other novelists. In " What is a Good Novel? " written in 1924, he remarks that a novelist must be unbiased and sympathetic or he will not get near the truth. And in his final significant statement on his art, " The Progress of the Novel," he affirms that the greatest novelists—Dostoevsky, Balzac—are those of great sympathies, that lesser artists—Joyce, Lawrence—possess less compassion, and that still lesser artists—Huxley—possess hostility and bitterness that are incompatible with great art (presumably because these are not understanding emotions) .

There is, when all is said and done, a genuine consistency

in Bennett's viewpoint, not merely consistency in a single
opinion held over the years of his literary career but—more
importantly—consistency of parts. He was, from first to last,
a realist in search of beauty, expecting to find beauty in
truth, crediting the shaping spirit of a compassionate imagination with its discovery. To the extent that he was a
realist in the conventional literary sense of the term, he
was employing a technique of limited usefulness in dis-
closing the hidden beauty of reality.

At least in print, Bennett never discussed esthetics or
his own craft except in very general terms. Probably he
felt that his proper task was to find beauty rather than to
explain it, that his art must speak for itself. The present
study has tried to assume that critical task. The preceding
chapters have discussed beauty. They have traced the unfolding of the mind of Sophia Baines, the movement toward
death of Henry Earlforward, the image that compels Edwin
Clayhanger. They have traced the curve of provincial history, the evolutionary cycle, the repeated patterns of human
destinies. These are things of beauty that lie hidden beneath
appearances, superficial details, isolated and unique events.
They are, perhaps, the sort of beauty that modern criticism
has the skills to expose. There is another aspect of beauty
in Bennett that the preceding chapters have not directly
approached, the sort which was once implied when an-
thologists made selections of " beauties of Shakespeare."
Such beauty belongs with Bennett's other beauties, but here
it will not so much be explained as be pointed to. For
this task a novel will serve that is commonly thought to be
an inferior work: *The Pretty Lady.*
    Walter Allen calls *The Pretty Lady* " cheap and sensa-
tional." Geoffrey West says it is " sentimental melodrama."
And Reginald Pound remarks that it is " one of a series

of rent-paying novels." But Georges Lafourcade calls it a great novel. And Bennett himself thought that it was " jolly well constructed." All of these opinions may be right. Certainly Bennett's is. The parallel plotting, elaborate imagery and symbolism, sophisticated character portrayal, etc., that have been explored in some of the other novels are displayed here with the same skill. These will not be examined.

The sensationalism in *The Pretty Lady* is not adequately indicated by its title. The heroine is a prostitute, but the lurid passages of the novel primarily concern maiming, slaughter, and suicide during the first World War: a child's severed arm lying in a London street after a Zeppelin raid, a girl's scalp torn off by a machine in a factory, the virtual suicide of one character during an air raid, and the threatened suicide of another character at the end of the novel. These accidents and acts occur in a sexually surcharged and tawdry atmosphere; the people involved in them are vulgar. At the same time, the two main characters are dull rather than sensational in their vulgarity, and their actions tend to reduce the lurid to the prosaic. They are quite proper people. Christine, the heroine, is no Nana. She serves no perversions in the course of the novel and does not so much as mention any; although she sleeps with many men, she is seen in relationships with only two, and in both instances the relationships are decidedly sentimental; she is devoutly religious and characteristically wears an attitude of demure innocence. Hoape, the hero, is an English gentleman; he thinks he has good manners, good taste, and right ideas; he is discreet, he conscientiously does his bit for the war with his right hand and accepts his war profits with his left. He and Christine contribute to the cheapness and sentimentality of the novel, but they mitigate its sensationalism.

By and large it must be said that although Bennett chooses a subject—wartime England—and characters that to a considerable extent determine the atmosphere of his novel, forcing it to be, in a way, cheap, sentimental, and melodramatic, he does not exploit these qualities for their own sake. Only the reader who confuses Bennett with his characters can think so.

The novel opens in the first months of World War I, when Christine has fled from Paris to London; it closes a couple of years later, when she has been abandoned by Hoape. Hoape, rather than Christine, is the central figure of the novel; he is seen in his liaison with her and in his relationships with two other women, society women, Queenie Paulle and Concepcion Smith, all of whom he at one time or another contemplates marrying; he is also seen in the conduct of his altruistic wartime activities. The action of the novel is episodic; there are few convolutions and no mysteries of plot; several scenes could be removed without breaking the narrative thread. The novel is not a patriotic novel in the sense that *Mr. Britling Sees It Through* is; it is in no sense a protest novel as *A Farewell to Arms* is. If the novel says anything, it says that the particular scene of London in World War I is very much like other scenes of death and love of other wars. If the novel rises above its scene, it does so by occasionally making the shabby and tawdry seem touching and beautiful.

There are, perhaps, a half dozen moments in the novel, some of them hardly scenes at all, that justify it. In the first of them Bennett presents an image of Hoape having his boots polished. The whole chapter in which the image appears is irrelevant to the narrative; but its religious overtones and some of its details, such the man rising from the earth and the act of polishing, bind it intimately to the major themes, scenes, and motifs of the novel. The image itself makes clear the distance that Bennett maintains from his hero; it suggests more powerfully than any other passage in his novels—with the possible exception of the Bastile scene in *Clayhanger*—where his social sympathies lay. The manager of the bootshop which Hoape (whose initials are G. J.) patronizes is a servile creature who treats Hoape as though he were God; when he sees that Hoape's boots need polishing, he recognizes a threat to God's perfection:

> . . . he went swiftly across to a speaking-tube and snapped: "Polisher!"
>
> A trap-door opened in the floor of the shop and a horrible, pallid, weak, cringing man came up out of the earth of St. James's, and knelt before God far more submissively than even the manager had knelt. He had brushes and blacking, and he blacked and he brushed and breathed alternately, undoing continually with his breath or his filthy hands what he had done with his brush. He never looked up, never spoke. When he had made the boots like mirrors he gathered together his implements and vanished, silent and dutifully bent, through the trap-door back into the earth of St. James's. And because the trap-door had not shut properly the manager stamped on it and stamped down the pale man definitely into the darkness underneath. And then G. J. was wafted out of the shop with smiles and bows.

Not a passage that one would point to in order to illustrate patient realism. Reality here is a vision. It is a vision of beauty, "the terrible beauty which hides itself in the ugliness of life" that Bennett found in *The Mummer's Wife*. The vision is seen at an esthetic distance not only from Hoape but also from the boot-polisher. Bennett's sympathies may be inferred but they are not stated: he believed that the artist fails who takes sides for and against his characters. At the same time, his distance is annihilated by love. He wrote in *The Author's Craft* (and said the same thing elsewhere throughout his writings) that whether the chief figure of a novel is a saint or a sinner, " the single motive that should govern the choice of a principal figure is the motive of love for that figure." Hoape is not condemned here, and he is cast in such a light elsewhere in the novel that some of its other beauties are associated with him.

Hoape leaves the bootshop to go to his club. It is morning on a day very early in the war. The war has hardly touched him. He sits in his club and listens to two armchair strategists, one of whom says, " Obviously the centre of gravity is no longer in the West—it's in the East. In the West, roughly, equilibrium has been established." Later in the morning he goes to the funeral of Lord Roberts in Westminster Abbey. He goes because only the select few can go; he goes in order to say he was there. But he is a sentimentalist, and once there he succumbs to the solemn pomp of the occasion. He nearly cries. He is uplifted. He becomes patriotic. He sees that he has a mission in the war: to be kind, to uphold the truth, to maintain his equanimity. His companion at the Abbey, a War Office official, reveals to him that Concepcion Smith, a society friend with whom Hoape plans to have lunch, has just lost her husband in the war. She has not yet been informed. Hoape sees that his immediate mission is to prepare her for the news in the kindest possible way. He goes to her.

Concepcion is one of the *nouveaux riches*; she is vulgar and vain; she is brazen and self-dramatizing. Nevertheless, she has some fragments of poetry in her (Shakespeare and Milton), and she possesses some wit. Hoape hardly knows how to fulfil his task; he talks about the war, retails the opinion that equilibrium has been established on the Western Front; he listens in desperation while she, who is a bride of a few weeks, tells him how she must steel herself for the possibility of her husband's death. When she says that she ought to prepare herself to the extent of ordering mourning clothes, he realizes that she is becoming hysterical, that she is suffering from the sexual loss of her husband. He is mistaken. She shows him a telegram from the War Office; it arrived a few minutes before him. He is shocked; he reproaches her, saying: " Why didn't you tell me at once? " She says:

"Couldn't. Besides, I had to see if I could stand it. Because I've got to stand it, G. J. . . . . And, moreover, in our set it's a sacred duty to be original."

She snatched the telegram, tore it in two, and pushed the pieces back into her gown.

" ' Poor wounded name! ' " she murmured, " ' my bosom as a bed shall lodge thee.' "

The next moment she fell to the floor, at full length on her back. G. J. sprang to her, kneeling on her rich, out-spread gown, and tried to lift her.

" No, no! " she protested faintly, dreamily, with a feeble frown on her pale forehead. " Let me lie. Equilibrium has been established on the Western Front."

This was her greatest *mot*.

No one will ever reread *The Pretty Lady* because he thinks G. J. and Concepcion are great characters; but he might reread it because he feels that in this moment their situation is touching and pathetic, that it is rendered beautiful. The occasion is melodramatic but at the same time restrained. The lines from *Two Gentlemen of Verona* (when Julia lodges Proteus's wounded name—a torn letter instead of a torn telegram—in her bosom) and the ironical allusion to Hoape's conversation at his club put the immediate crisis at some distance. For Concepcion, the distance is fugue;

for the reader, it is control. Bennett closes off the melo-drama abruptly with the final line, which ends the chapter.

This early scene in the novel is echoed in two later scenes. During an air raid Hoape is visiting another society friend, Queenie Paulle. Unlike Concepcion, Queenie comes from an old family. She is a vulgar, vicious, and reckless woman. The one hint of sexual perversion in the novel concerns Queenie rather than Christine: when Hoape remarks to Concepcion that Queenie ought to be whipped for her recklessness, Concepcion, who is knowledgeable about the sexual vagaries of her friends, replies dryly, " She'd like nothing better." Queenie goes out on the roof of her mansion to watch the raid and will not come in at Hoape's command.

> . . . she easily escaped him. He saw the whiteness of her skirt in the distance of the roof, dimly rising. She was climbing the ladder up the side of the chimney. She stood on the top of the chimney and laughed again. A gun sounded.

Hoape goes inside. He talks with Concepcion, who tells him that Queenie loves him. She quotes Milton to him on the relationship of the sexes. A servant runs in to say that Queenie has been killed. Concepcion, who perhaps loves Queenie too dearly, is prostrated, but not until she makes another *mot*. Months later Hoape visits Concepcion in a country town to which she has retired after a nervous break-down. Much in the manner of her earlier telling him that she was going to order mourning clothes for her husband's death, she tells him now that she is making her will: she intends to commit suicide. He says:

> " What do you want to do it for? What's happened? "
> " Then you believe I mean to do it? "
> " Yes," he replied sincerely, and as naturally as he could.

" That's the tone I like to hear," said she, smiling.

" I felt sure I could count on you not to indulge in too much nonsense. Well, I'm going to try the next avatar just to remind fate of my existence. I think fate's forgotten me, and I can stand anything but that. I've lost Carly, and I've lost Queen. . . . Oh, G. J.! Isn't it awful to think that when I offered you Queen she'd already gone, and it was only her dead body I was offering you? . . . And I've lost my love. And I've failed, and I shall never be any more good here. I swore I would see a certain thing through, and I haven't seen it through, and I can't! But I've told you all this before. . . . What's left? Even my unhappiness is leaving me. Unless I kill myself I shall cease to exist. Don't you understand? Yes, you do."

The lines ring true to Concepcion's character. The pathos is true. Hoape, who at the beginning of the novel thought his first mission in the war was to help her stand the loss of her husband, now sees that he must save her from suicide. He is contemplating his virtue as the novel ends.

Perhaps these fragments, despite being out of context, suggest something of the beauty that *The Pretty Lady* possesses. More often than not, that beauty is mournful rather than terrible. So Christine describes it in the opening chapter of the novel. She is in the Promenade of a West End theatre. On stage is a gaudy and indecent revue; in the darkness sits an audience that watches lasciviously yet restrains itself and that in its ordinary public life refuses to acknowledge the reality of which the revue speaks. Behind the audience is the Promenade; it is this which the revue mirrors; it is this which the revue, however daring, only palely imitates. Yet the Promenade itself, to Christine, who is Latin, is constrained. She observes these Northerners: " With scarcely an exception they all had the same strange look, the same absence of gesture." She thinks to herself, " My God! How mournful it is! "

Her exclamation is unsophisticated. More than anything else it expresses her anxiety at being at a strange place in a foreign country. But for the reader it is an accurate description of the pervasive quality of the novel, the quality that underlies the tawdriness and melodrama. Insofar as the novel concerns war and death, such a quality is to be expected. At the same time—as the opening chapter suggests—mournfulness pervades the novel as an expression of a judgment upon the human condition, of which war is simply a manifestation. Bennett has looked at the superficial facts of life, seen beneath them a mournful beauty, and tried to convey it. Much of the mournfulness has nothing directly to do with the war, and some of it is artificial, formal. Thus the funeral of Lord Roberts in Westminster Abbey, although inherently a mournful occasion, is mournful also because of the architecture of the Abbey. Here Bennett draws upon someone else's conception of the human condition, expressed architecturally; and appropriately enough he tries to capture the quality of the Abbey impressionistically rather than realistically:

> The procession, headed by the clergy, moved slowly, amid the vistas ending in the dull burning of stained glass, through the congregation in mourning and in khaki, through the lines of yellow-glowing candelabra, towards the crowd of scarlet under the dome; the summit of the dome was hidden in soft mist.

Thus the ending of the novel, although sad in its depiction of a hapless woman, is mournful also because of the slow rhythm that Bennett gives to the passage. Hoape has just caught a glimpse of Christine on the street. He thinks that she is importuning men, that she has sunk to a level in her profession that she previously had scorned; and since he himself has been providing for her, he believes that she must be depraved. His reasoning merely serves his newly aroused desire to turn his attention upon Concepcion. Christine is searching for a soldier whom she has been mothering for some time. A deeply religious person, recently returned to Catholicism, she believes that the Virgin Mary brought the soldier to her and thinks that the soldier has been calling to her. (Once before in the novel, while she was in a restaurant, she heard his voice and ran out into the street and found him, although as far as she knew he was in France.) The passage is not an example of realistic prose; it tries to convey stylistically the mournful beauty beneath the surface of life.

> How in his human self-sufficiency could he be expected to know that he had judged the negligible Christine unjustly? Was he divine that he could see in the figure of the wanton who peered at soldiers in the street a self-convinced mystic envoy of the most clement Virgin, an envoy passionately repentant after apostasy, bound at all costs to respond to an imagined voice long unheard, and seeking—though in vain this second time—the protégé of the Virgin so that she might once more succour and assuage his affliction?

The Pretty Lady presents a very partial conception of human existence. No novel can do more. Even to the extent that it presents the conception of a single man, it offers a very partial one. For Bennett was not a man who suffered continually from *weltschmerz*. One of the impressive things about his serious novels is that each of them presents a different perspective of the human condition. To be sure, there are certain philosophical commitments that run through all of them (such as the belief in evolution), just as there are recognizable techniques that characterize his approach. But *The Pretty Lady* offers a view of the human condition different from that of *The Glimpse* or *Riceyman Steps* or *Lord Raingo* or *Imperial Palace*; just as *Clayhanger* offers a different view from that of *The Old Wives' Tale*. It is apparent that some of the works of the greatest novelists are little more than repetitions of previous works, setting new characters to dance to an old tune. To make a particularly invidious comparison, *To the Lighthouse* is very much the same novel as *Mrs. Dalloway*—much as one may admire both of them. Dickens, James, Conrad, and others can be pointed to. Bennett himself in *The Author's Craft* remarks upon "the creative repetition to which all novelists—including the most powerful—are reduced." But in a clear way his novels do not repeat themselves; he was not content, when he achieved fame with *The Old Wives' Tale*, to maintain his fame with a succession of imitations. If his novels can be said to be repetitious in a significant way, it is that they all attempt to reveal some new facet of hidden beauty. In the closing passage of *The Truth about An Author*, written very early in his career, he looks forward (accurately, as it turned out) to another thirty years of novel-writing, and he sees his works as "interminable variations on the theme of beauty." *The Pretty Lady* is a mournful variation.

CHAPTER 7

Philosophical Detachment and the Savor of Life

THE OLD WIVES' TALE

IMPERIAL PALACE

IN HIS PREFACE to *The Old Wives' Tale* Bennett remarks that a friend of his, whose judgment he respected, thought that the novel "was honest but dull, and that when it was not dull it had a regrettable tendency to facetiousness." Two recent critics, William M. Crockett and Thomas J. Roberts, take favorable notice of the novel's facetiousness. But generally the facetiousness has either been ignored or gone unrecognized. From an early American critic, who considered that the novel might have been improved by some comic relief, to E. M. Forster ("strong, sincere, sad"), Lafourcade ("classical tragedy"), and E. M. W. Tillyard ("a successful rendering of a choric feeling, the feeling of provincial puritanism"), Bennett's critics have usually been concerned with its serious intentions. The serious intentions color the facetiousness: the humor in the novel—pervasive in the first two books—is a grave humor. It reflects an attitude toward the human situation that is at once compassionate and detached.

Consider the opening lines of the novel:

> Those two girls, Constance and Sophia Baines, paid no
> heed to the manifold interest of their situation, of which,

indeed, they had never been conscious. They were, for example, established almost precisely on the fifty-third parallel of latitude. A little way to the north of them, in the creases of a hill famous for its religious orgies, rose the river Trent, the calm and characteristic stream of middle England. Somewhat further northwards, in the near neighborhood of the highest public-house in the realm, rose two lesser rivers, the Dane and the Dove, which, quarreling in early infancy, turned their backs on each other, and the one by favour of the Weaver and the other by favour of the Trent, watered between them the whole width of England, and poured themselves respectively into the Irish Sea and the German Ocean. What a county of modest, unnoticed rivers!

The information on the fifty-third parallel might at first blush be taken as an entirely serious observation by a realist; but the juxtaposition of orgies and a calm stream, of a high public house and quarreling streams, suggests irony; and the metaphor of the division of the Dane and the Dove is playful.

Bennett's humor is more obvious in the account of John Baines that ends the first section of the chapter. Mr. Baines lost the signboard of his shop in a gale and never replaced it. He hated " puffing."

> Uninformed persons who wished to find Baines's must ask and learn. For Mr. Baines to have replaced the sign would have been to condone, yea, to participate in, the modern craze for unscrupulous self-advertisement. This abstention of Mr. Baines's from indulgence in signboards was somehow accepted by the more thoughtful members of the community as evidence that the height of Mr. Baines's principles was greater even than they had imagined.
>
> Constance and Sophia were the daughters of this credit to human nature. . . .

No doubt Baines is a credit to human nature; no doubt Sophia in that later scene in which she puts a defeat upon

Gerald Scales draws upon "generations of honest living."
Bennett stands with the Baineses against the unscrupulous
self-advertisers who occupy their shop at the end of the
novel and against unscrupulous young lovers. But Bennett
is amused by John Baines's vanity, just as he is amused by
the theft by which Sophia preserves her honesty.

Two of the most delightful passages in Book One of the
novel concern incidental religious figures. The Reverend
Mr. Murley is offered gratis a new suit of clothes by the
pious John Baines: "Mr. Murley, who had a genuine
medieval passion for souls, and who spent his money and
health freely in gratifying the passion, had accepted the offer
strictly on behalf of Christ, and had carefully explained to
Mr. Povey Christ's use for multifarious pockets." And
Archibald Jones, celebrated religious intellectual, whose
Christian name "was a luscious, resounding mouthful for
admirers," has a love affair with a dessicated spinster: "It
must be a union of intellects! He had been impressed by
hers, and she by his, and then their intellects had kissed.
Within a week fifty thousand women in forty counties had
pictured to themselves this osculation of intellects, and
shrugged their shoulders, and decided once more than men
were incomprehensible." Small wonder that the *Contemporary Review* has published articles on Bennett's failure to
describe Wesleyan Methodism accurately!

This humor is never merely a relief from the prosaic and
tragic; it gives unique color to them. It represents an unmistakable perspective. There are few passages in the novel,
even of the most somber cast, that do not have their under-
current of humor. Consider John Baines's death in Book
One. He slides from his bed and is asphyxiated while
Sophia leaves him for a few minutes to flirt with Gerald.
Mr. Critchlow, Baines's close friend, suspects the truth:
"'Gallivanting with that young Scales!' said Mr. Critchlow,

with devilish ferocity. ' Well, you've killed yer father; that's all! ' " And then Mrs. Baines appears on the scene, and she and Critchlow go into the bedroom to look at John Baines:

> They knew not that they were gazing at a vanished era. John Baines had belonged to the past, to the age when men really did think of their souls, when orators by phrases could move crowds to fury or to pity, when no one had learnt to hurry, when Demos was only turning in his sleep, when the sole beauty of life resided in its inflexible and slow dignity, when hell really had no bottom, and a gilt-clasped Bible really was the secret of England's greatness. Mid-Victorian England lay on that mahogany bed. Ideals had passed away with John Baines. It is thus that ideals die; not in the conventional pageantry of honoured death, but sorrily, ignobly, while one's head is turned—

This is strong, sincere and sad. John Baines is a credit to human nature. It would appear that there is no humor, only a somber irony. But then the last line: " while one's head is turned." Does it refer to Sophia's having gone out of the room? Does it refer to her head being turned by Gerald, to her choosing, implicitly, the code of a younger age? Or does it refer to John Baines's head " hanging, inverted, near the floor between the bed and the ottoman "? In any event, Sophia seems to have killed her father. If there is humor, it is savage, sardonic. But Bennett will not have Sophia kill her father; he immediately shifts from the Baineses to Gerald Scales: " The real murderer was having his dinner in the commercial room up at the Tiger, opposite the Town Hall."

Bennett's humor varies with his subject. The marvelously funny birthday party for young Cyril in Book Two is something quite different from the pathetically ironical departure of Mrs. Baines at the end of Book One (" She, a Syme of Axe! "). But all of the humor speaks for a man who is at once very close to and detached from his characters. He possesses the compassion to see their lives as they themselves see them, and he possesses the detachment to see their lives under the aspect of a materialistic eternity. And certainly the characteristic expression of this complex viewpoint in *The Old Wives' Tale* is a grave humor. Especially at the end this is the dominant quality, and it lingers in the mind. Sophia has come home and died. Constance has died. The Baines shop has been sold. Nothing is left. The story has been told. But Bennett has space for a sardonic comment by Charles Critchlow, who comes to Constance's funeral and says, "It's a pity her didn't live long enough to hear as Federation is going on after all! That would ha' worritted her." And space to describe the old dog Fossette going reluctantly to its supper, conscious of neglect: "She glanced at the soup-plate, and, on the chance that it might after all contain something worth inspection, she awkwardly balanced herself on her old legs and went to it again."

Perhaps in time *The Old Wives' Tale* may seem to be a semicomic novel.* Eventually the perspective that produced it may seem close to that of an earlier English realist, Henry Fielding. If the time comes, critics will note that Bennett wrote several expressly comic novels and plays and that he produced one of the best of them, *Buried Alive* (a work that is superior to the better known *The Card*), during a short interlude in the composition of *The Old Wives' Tale.* Such a shift in opinion will afford an interesting contrast to another shift, that concerning George Peele's *The Old Wives' Tale.*

---

* In an unpublished letter of April 2, 1907, to his literary agent, J. B. Pinker, Bennett wrote: "I shall then do a very long serious novel, which will contain a great deal of humor as well as of tragedy." He began *The Old Wives' Tale* in October.

According to David Horne in *The Life and Minor Works
of George Peele*, the Elizabethan play was until recently
regarded as a burlesque of romantic comedy but now is
regarded as a serious romantic comedy with bits of satire
in it. Peele's work offers the rudiments of a play within a
play. Three pages who are lost in the woods are invited
to spend the night at the home of Clunch the Smith. His
wife Madge tells two of them her " old wives' winter's tale "
about magicians and charms and enchantments. The characters in the tale appear on the scene to play their roles.
When the tale is done, it is morning, and Madge invites
her guests to breakfast.

In Bennett's *The Old Wives' Tale*, which concerns two
young girls who become old wives, Constance and Sophia
at the beginning are looking down from a window upon
a play, the servant Maggie's quest for romance: " Engage-
ments and tragic partings were Maggie's pastime." Then
Constance and Sophia themselves step into the frame to
enact their play. It is not a ludicrous play, like Maggie's.
But it is a romantic comedy, with its own magicians and
enchantments: " The most commonplace occurrence! The
eternal cause had picked up a commercial traveller [Gerald
Scales] . . . and endowed him with all the glorious, unique,
incredible attributes of a god, and planted him down before
Sophia in order to produce the eternal effect. A miracle
performed specially for Sophia's benefit! " The event is
commonplace. It remains commonplace even after one
realizes that Bennett is playing upon another play with his
image of the god Gerald planted down upon the stage: the
Greek play, with its *deux ex machina*. The whole story,
the whole novel, is commonplace. Ordinary things happen
in it. Nothing happens to Constance and Sophia about
which the reader could not say: that could have happened
to me. Yet on the last day of her life Sophia looks back

over forty years and makes a transforming judgment: " It is monstrous, and I cannot stand it." That is what life is for her. Ordinary life. And so the story ends: Constance and Sophia die and step out of the scene that once they were looking upon. The framework remains, just as it does in the Peele play. So a servant gives a dog its meal; the smith's wife gives the pages a meal. Curious! But then Bennett knew Peele.

Bennett's detachment makes him a humorist. He takes none of his characters with complete seriousness. It becomes clear that the complex religious allusions in *The Price of Love* are to be taken with a smile. The gas lamp in the sitting room is not really " like the moon in heaven! " The exclamation point gives the game away. Louis Fores is not a " superior being." He merely suffers from human vanity. But Bennett is not simply detached from his characters; he is detached from the reality that they represent, whether the reality is Staffordshire or London. On the same basis he would not take Christ entirely seriously. The edge cuts both ways. Louis Fores may seem all the more absurd through the metaphor by which he is described; but messiahs, too, are absurd. They are not superior beings. Bennett believes that the needs, fears, and desires which produce religious leaders, religious dogmas, are very much akin to those that produce the sorts of people and the conduct of life that he describes in *The Price of Love.*

His detachment is not a withdrawal from life. It is the attitude of a man who at the same time possesses a Christ-like compassion for people, and who possesses a great love for life. The paradox is easy to accept. One is inclined to think that those who take life lightly are those who can savor it fully. What is clearer than that the zealot who wants to reform the world has a hatred of life? " What a

crew! " exclaimed Bennett (who was a socialist) about
communists in a day when young British intellectuals were
beginning to think about saving the world. Yet, as the history of the last thirty years has shown, the paradox is easiest
to acknowledge when one is detached; the lesson of the
French Revolution is more obvious than the lesson one is
learning in life. And Bennett's mingled detachment and
savoring of life have not been well received in a cultural
community that since World War I has been inclined to
take a more serious view of life. The pessimism which
characterizes the *avant garde* of the twenties and the political purposefulness which characterizes that of the thirties
and forties are foreign to Bennett's outlook. Critics have
recognized the seriousness of *The Old Wives' Tale*; they
have been offended by the frivolity of *Imperial Palace*,
which deals with a luxury hotel. In those realms where
their sympathies lie, they have seen Bennett's sympathies;
in other realms they have seen an artist succumbing to
vulgarity.

Geoffrey West, whose *The Problem of Arnold Bennett*
was published in the thirties, discusses the seriousness of
The Old Wives' Tale. The book possesses " an unfailing
sense of the human tragedy of time and change." Bennett's
mood is " severely repressed." His outlook is " pessimistic."
The work is notable for its " honesty " and " compassion."
Then West turns to *Imperial Palace*: " What the *hell*, one
is irritably driven to ask, does it matter whether Gracie . . .
orders beer or brandy or lemonade or methylated spirit so
long as she gets what she wants! . . . If the luxury hotel is,
as a character suggests and Bennett by taking it as his subject
seems to agree, one of the most *characteristic* creations of
modern civilization, then so much the worse for civilization." Yet Gracie's ordering sherry in a London pub [she
is a rich and beautiful girl; she is slumming] ought to be

no less interesting than Sophia Scales's drinking champagne
in a Paris restaurant. Gracie could be as much an object
of compassion as Sophia. Bennett is interested in both girls,
he has compassion for both, he also laughs at both. He
possesses detachment and an interest in the frivolity of
modern London as well as in that of nineteenth-century
Paris and the Midlands. That attitude is at the heart of
Imperial Palace.

Explanations for the " failure " of *Imperial Palace* assume
a variety of forms and reflect complex and varying viewpoints. One of the commonest explanations—in which
Imperial Palace serves mainly as an illustration—is that with
the inexplicable exception of *Riceyman Steps* Bennett never
wrote well about anything except the Five Towns. The
Five Towns, it is argued, he wrote about with the sureness
of complete understanding; they were in his bones; whereas
Paris and London he saw superficially from a Duval Restaurant and the Grill Room of the Savoy Hotel. There is
an important objection to this viewpoint. Bennett left the
Potteries as a raw young man of twenty-one and rarely
returned. He did have one or two friends in the district,
and he returned on occasion to gather material for his
books (in quite the same manner as when he visited the
Savoy Hotel to gather material for *Imperial Palace*) . But
by and large he had as little to do with the place as possible.
Inexplicably, then, not the raw youth but the mature man
conceived *The Old Wives' Tale*; inexplicably he did so
while sitting in a Duval Restaurant looking at a French
woman. One may say, as J. B. Priestley does in his Introduction to *The Old Wives' Tale*, that by leaving the Five
Towns Bennett gained detachment, and so was able to
understand them better. This will help to explain *The
Old Wives' Tale*, just as D. H. Lawrence's leaving the Mid-

lands will help to explain *Sons and Lovers.* But then there is *Riceyman Steps,* just as there is *Kangaroo.* And *Imperial Palace.*

There are other explanations for the supposed failure of *Imperial Palace.* They range from the opinion that journalism consumed most of Bennett's energies during his later years to the opinion that a death wish consumed them. These will be considered in Appendix A.

It is certain that Bennett was fascinated by the hotel life that is described in *Imperial Palace.* One of his earliest novels, *The Grand Babylon Hotel,* has a hotel for its setting; another one, *Hugo,* employs a similar organism, a department store. In an essay written in 1910, " Hotel on the Landscape," Bennett calls hotels "the sole genuine contribution made by the modern epoch to the real history of architecture," an opinion that he has Sir Henry Savott echo in *Imperial Palace.* And just as he wrote about the gestation of *The Old Wives' Tale* that "for several years I looked it squarely in the face at intervals, and then walked away to write novels of smaller scope," so he wrote about the gestation of *Imperial Palace* that "I have been fighting for years against the instinct to write this particular novel." There are various reasons for his fascination. A general interest in architecture was surely prominent. The pages of his *Journal* are studded with his responses to the architecture of many countries. His closest friend for many years was the architect E. A. Rickards. The architectural ambitions of Edwin Clayhanger and the architectural achievements of George Cannon in *The Roll-Call* reflect the fact that in his own youth Bennett wanted to be an architect. Another reason was his sociological bent: a novelist who was interested in seeing life could hardly ignore a characteristic feature of contemporary society. Another reason must have been his artistic interest in microcosms, his artistic need for unity of place—an interest and need like Kafka's and Mann's. Another must have been his predisposition in the conduct of his own life toward the clear organization and efficiency that he could observe in a well-run hotel.

At the same time, he regarded hotel life with detachment, sometimes with revulsion. In a letter to his nephew Richard, he remarks of a New Year's Eve party at the Savoy, the model for *Imperial Palace* (the remark is paralleled in a *Journal* entry) :

> The New Year's Eve dinner at the Savoy was the noisiest, vulgarest, costliest thing of the sort I ever had anything to do with. I had scarcely imagined that there were so many people in London with so much money and so little taste. However, I got all the material I wanted. . . .

The material was for *Mr Prohack*, then being written, but appears to have been only partly used in the dinner scene at the Grand Babylon Hotel. Years later it probably provided the substance of the chapter " New Year's Eve " in *Imperial Palace*. Presumably Bennett would have agreed with Geoffrey West's denunciation:

> The entire thing, as he [Bennett] draws it, is directed to the service of a vulgar, competitive, unproductive, sexual existence; there is scarcely one person concerned in it who serves a really *necessary* need.

The paradox requires analysis.

Is luxury ethically justifiable? This is one way to phrase the central theme of the novel; it is approximately what Evelyn Orcham asks at the end of the book: " Were luxury hotels sociologically justifiable? " Evelyn gives his answer: " He didn't know. He couldn't decide. He knew merely that he was going straight on. He said to himself: ' There's a lot of things in this world you'll never get the hang of.

And only idiots try.' " Evelyn is a naïve man; he is an instrument but not the sole voice of Bennett's argument.

Bennett makes his argument difficult for himself. The Imperial Palace is the *ne plus ultra* of luxury. For its guests—who never seem aught but American tobacco millionaires, Oriental potentates, and English lords of finance, along with their respective Puritanical wives, harems, and society queens—the hotel satisfies many whims and condones others: parties at 3 A. M., unusual furnishings specially built or obtained upon request, destructive rampages by drunken actresses, etc. The hotel's cuisine is perhaps the best in the world, and its entertainments are extraordinarily expensive and vulgar. The code of the hotel is such that when a drunken, thieving guest provokes an employee into an argument, Evelyn tells his head housekeeper, " There can't be any such thing as provocation in this hotel. . . . There never has been before, and there mustn't be again. If the customer is Judas Iscariot, he's still the customer till he's safely outside the hotel." In a word, the hotel is the lackey of capitalism; it caters to the parasitism and corruption of the modern aristocracy of wealth.

Evelyn sometimes regards his guests and his financial associates in his hotel enterprise in the most cynical terms. The latter " take as a right all they can get . . ."; " he disdained them as a greedy, grasping and soulless crew," " parasites on the industry." The former make of the Imperial Palace " a den of well-dressed thieves." When Evelyn and Gracie visit the Caligula restaurant, whose name implies its character, he reflects that the guests of the Imperial Palace are no different from the " grotesquely indecent . . . old men " and the " hard, insincere, grasping . . . girls " he sees here. How does the luxury world redeem itself?

An answer of sorts is given in the continuation of Evelyn's reflections at the Caligula. Despite his admission of similarity, he is revolted by the immediate scene in a way that he is not revolted by the spectacle of the Imperial Palace. He asks Gracie why she likes to come to such a place; and when she replies that she wants to see everything and that here one learns about human nature, he responds grimly, "Some sorts of human nature." Her answer to this is decisive: "Aren't we all God's creatures?" A few minutes later, when Gracie expresses some distaste for two Lesbians, Evelyn repeats her phrase just as decisively. At a much earlier point in the novel, when in the middle of the night Evelyn makes the rounds of his hotel, he thinks: "Salt of the earth, these wealthy residents in the largest and most luxurious luxury hotel on earth, deferentially served by bowing waiters, valets, maids! They pressed magic buttons, and their caprices were instantly gratified. But . . . they were as touching as the piteous figures crouching and shivering in the lamp-lit night on the benches of the Thames Embankment."

Another inadequate answer is given in the personal conduct of Evelyn and his subordinates in the parasitic and corrupt world they serve. Their gospel is work and their devotion conscionable—both within the limits of human frailty. As the book opens, Evelyn is seen at 4 A. M. rising for a day's work; he has a long day that takes him up to midnight, and he rises again for an hour in the middle of the night. Such a day is unusual; ordinarily Evelyn limits his day so as to obtain six hours of sleep at night. The hotel is his life; it has been his life during the twenty years of his widowerhood and probably before; it will likely remain his *raison d'être*. The action of the novel represents a crisis or an interlude, when his gospel is challenged by his sexual needs. Upon first seeing Gracie Savott he thinks, "work first, career first, women second, even were she another Helen"; then he is smitten by her and deserts his hotel for two days of lovemaking. "Be sure your sin will find you out," he reflects upon the second day of their idyll, thinking not of sexual sin but of sin against his hotel. The two sins do intertwine. "Duty before—love," he tells Gracie, and he returns to his work. Later he succumbs to the more solid attractions of Violet Powler, but it is notable that in the nine days following their betrothal—the nine days of the end of the book—he sees her only twice, briefly. His thought at the end of the book, "was Violet, or the perfecting of luxury hotels throughout Europe, his life-work?," is a transitory doubt as to his commitment to the latter. (The similarity between his confused feelings for both Gracie and Violet suggests this.) At the point when Evelyn is returning to the hotel from his days in Paris with Gracie, with his struggle between work and love unresolved, Bennett writes: "The new Evelyn saw the hotel . . . in a mist, which no effort could dispel. Whereas Gracie would appear out of the mist with all the solid and detailed reality of life itself. His interest in the Palace was not authentic." The image, ambiguous in implication, is of Venus rising from the sea. Evelyn has seen the image before: when he first goes to the Laundry and sees Violet Powler ("Aphrodite springing from the hot dampness of the Laundry") and when he reflects upon his conquest of Gracie ("thinking to himself: 'By God! By God!' Meaning that he had done it, had voyaged to Cythera"). Gracie in fact emerges from the sea at the opening of the novel, having come to the hotel from her "cockle-shell the 'Caractacus'" that has just crossed the ocean from New York. Love and work are synonymous to Evelyn.

Violet Powler is in a similar way devoted to her work for the Imperial Palace. Before coming to the hotel proper, she has worked a fifty-five-hour week at the Laundry; in her new role as housekeeper she works a sixty to seventy-hour

week and exults in it. "She never felt fatigue, nor bore-
dom. . . . She went to bed with reluctance, and arose joyous
and eager to start the new, long day. She found a grim
satisfaction in overworking both the loyal Mrs. Oulsnam
and the equally loyal Agatha." Evelyn is a surprised man
when after their betrothal Violet informs him that she
expects to desert housekeeping at the hotel for housekeeping
at home. Work is possibly synonymous with love for her too.

The moral quality of work at the Imperial Palace pervades the novel. Jack Cradock, the meat buyer, regards
the hotel as " sacred " and its manager as " a fellow-devotee
of honesty in a world only passably honest." The characteristic pose of the several housekeepers is with hands
folded in front of them, "nunlike." The tale of Alice
Brury's quarrelling with the drunken thief puts " shame
on every face "; for the personnel know that " the hotel
turns the other cheek every time." The suggestion by one
of the other housekeepers that Sir Henry Savott has had his
suite moved in order to be near Violet makes Violet feel
" as though she could never be clean again." Evelyn thinks
about his employees: " The Palace was their world and
their religion; its pre-eminence their creed, its welfare their
supreme aim. They respected and adored Evelyn. He was
their god. Or . . . the Palace was the god." The characteristic attitude of department heads is one of " benevolence ";
the desideratum in atmosphere is " tranquility." Of course,
the ideal is no more perfectly realized in the Imperial
Palace than—say—within the Catholic or Protestant Church.
But just as the Church holds itself aloof from crimes and
errors committed in its name or under its roof, so does the
Palace.

There is another partial answer. The hotel guests are
not entirely what they seem sometimes to Evelyn and his
fellow workers. On the evening of the first day, Evelyn
thinks of Gracie:

> Surely in the wide world that night there could not be any-
> thing to beat her! Idle, luxurious, rich, but a masterpiece!
> Maintained in splendour by the highly skilled and expensive
> labour of others, materially useless to society, yet she justified
> herself by her mere appearance. And she knew it, and her
> conscience was clear.

He is wrong in part but does not know it. Later, when he
is with her in Paris, he expresses a similar thought to her:

> You've got to go on being rich and spectacular and all that.
> It's not a bad thing, really. Has its uses in what political
> journalists call the fabric of society. We others are entitled
> to have something to look at. . . . In any case it's not the
> slightest use selling all you have and giving to the poor,
> or trying to do jobs that plain ordinary girls can do ten
> times better than you ever could.

What prompts these latter remarks is Gracie's discontent-
ment, her desire to work, and her desire to learn. In this
dual world of acolytes and parasites—all feeding on the host,
which is Evelyn or the hotel—Gracie is one of the most
serious persons, perhaps the most literate, and probably
the most honest. At the outset of the novel Gracie undertakes her " new life," which is to write a book. Coincidental
with her new life is the attempted suicide of her pregnant
maid, for whom subsequently Gracie is like a " mother to a
mother." She feels unsure that she can carry through the
writing of her book, and at one point decides to give it up,
and Evelyn believes at one point that she will not finish it.
Nevertheless she does and publishes the book pseudonym-
ously, so as not to trade on her name as friend Nancy
Penkethman does with her journalism. Gracie reads the
Bible, Shakespeare, Sir Arthur Eddington, Eric Remarque.
She reads passionately; she alone among the characters seeks
a purpose and meaning of life. Her search is superficial,

but it is earnest, perhaps desperate. In the title of her book, *Ideas and Sensations*, are named the two aspects of her learning. Her chief idea—to infer the contents of her book from her conversations with Evelyn—is the infinite, all-embracing quality of God, and hence the perfect unity and coherence of all animate and inanimate matter:

> If the divine creative mind is infinite, we are *it*. You and me, and all those people there. And these chairs and the lights from the chandelier. Everything. No getting away from it. You know the electrons, whirling around. Of course they aren't the purest form of the divine mind, I mean the first original form. But some finer kinds of electrons are—that our electrons are made of. Must be. And they're everywhere and they're all the same and all perfect and all working together, doing evolution.

In such a scheme luxury hotels have their place. Gracie's chief idea justifies her attitude toward sensations, her willingness to accept freely the physical world as well as the spiritual: "Aren't we all [even the hedonistic, the most depraved] God's creatures?" The ascetic and the acolyte are on a par with the voluptuary and the parasite.

Gracie's honesty is impressive. Though there are ambiguity and perversity in her behavior beyond the depths of her honesty, still her honesty is impressive. Within an hour after meeting Evelyn, "She persuaded herself that he knew all her thoughts. By a shameless secret act, she tried to strip her mind to him, tear off every rag of decency, expose it to him, nude." That night she and Evelyn and others watch the voluptuous dancing of Volivia in the restaurant. Evelyn (for whom "for years women had been his secret preoccupation") tells himself that he is not interested in the brazen display, yet he is compelled to watch it. Sir Henry Savott remarks in a diffident tone that two male

assistants are better. Gracie says, " it was shameless," and
then, " I loved it for being shameless. . . . What's the matter
with the flesh anyway? Don't we all know what we are? "

It is in the Paris chapters that Gracie's honesty, her baring
her soul to Evelyn, most clearly contrasts with Evelyn's dishonesty, his dissembling to himself and to her. It is she who
first acknowledges their mutual passion, she who directs
it to fruition, she who first speaks of their essential incom-
patibility, she who has the courage to make the break
between them. Immoral or perverse she may be in her
sensualism; but her desires are much less secret than
Evelyn's, and her understanding of their relationship is
much less clouded than his. Moreover, her sensualism is
fruitful: upon her break with Evelyn she marries Leo
Cheddar, and at the end of the novel she is pregnant.

The other important guest of the hotel is Gracie's father,
Sir Henry Savott, millionaire and financier. In his name,
capitalism is on exhibition and on trial. He is a large share-
holder in the company that owns the Caractacus, the ship
which has brought him and Gracie to England at the outset
of the novel and which in passage has developed a three-
inch split across the observation deck. There have been only
rumors of the disaster, and Evelyn reflects sardonically that
the press will not touch the story: " The four-million pound
crack was protected by the devoted adherence of the press
to the dogma that transatlantic liners are perfect. And
let no one breathe a word concerning the relation between
editors and advertisement-managers." Luxury liners are like
hotels, churches, and gods. Evelyn has the passing thought
that the publication of such a story would not only damage
transatlantic travel but his own hotel business, which is in
large part international. Then a couple of weeks later
Evelyn learns that despite efforts by the ship's company
to buy people's silence, a London newspaper will publish

the story. Immerson, the hotel's publicity manager, tells
Evelyn that he suspects that Savott is at the bottom of it:
he is unloading his own shares amid falling prices that will
plunge further with the publication of the story and then
will buy in again, standing to make a couple of hundred
thousand pounds by the maneuver. Savott denies insti-
gating the newspaper account but freely admits to the
selling and buying. " And why not? " he asks. Evelyn, who
had been revolted by Savott's possible machinations with
the newspaper, sanctions Immerson's plans to counter the
newspaper story by a plant in another newspaper—Immerson being concerned about the effects of the first story upon
the hotel business. Finally, when Savott righteously de-
nounces the " reptile press " at large for refusing to divulge
the ship disaster and points out to Evelyn that the second
story appeared too late to gain its desired effect, Evelyn
thinks:

> The great man [Savott] had not sinned. He had behaved as
> any speculative investor would behave. He had not broken
> the code. . . . And even if he had been at the bottom of it
> [the newspaper story], what then? He had not departed
> from the truth. The details were indisputable. The deck
> had split. Indeed, by smashing the agelong Fleet Street . . .
> hush-hush about Atlantic liners, the great man . . . had done
> good.

For the reader, there is no reason to exonerate Savott and
not enough evidence to condemn him. In the whole situation there is more evidence to condemn Evelyn.

In the matter of the proposed merger of the Imperial
Palace with other hotels under Savott's control, Savott
stands as the defender of the capitalistic faith. To Evelyn,
who is initially unsympathetic to the scheme and suggests
that " this mania for mergers . . . mean[s] the destroying

of individuality," Savott has several replies: (1) The merger "would mean the extension of *your* individuality." (2) Nothing can stop mergers:

> They've come, everywhere, in everything. They're still coming, and they'll keep on coming more and more. They're bound to. All big enterprises will get bigger, and small enterprises will be swallowed up. . . . I'm not a scientist, and I couldn't make a very clear story of evolution. But I've got the hang of it. And what I say is, the merger is evolution.

(3) Money isn't his motive but rather instinct:

> I'm interested in money, but I'm more interested in my instincts. . . . If they lead me to money, I can't help that. . . . I'm pushing evolution forward.

(4) Not only the top dogs will extend their individualities in merger enterprises:

> Mergers mean mass-production and lower prices. What's the matter with this country is that there isn't enough mass-production. Mass-production is the only chance for the under-dog, as far as I can see. . . . There is a chance that mass-production and machinery will abolish the under-dog. There's no other chance.

The merger goes through, and evolution is served; and some of the participants think that in the process " the astute Sir Henry might have gotten gains which no inquiry could ever disclose." Again Bennett leaves the reader in doubt: is Savott's reasoning valid or confused, honest or corrupt? One thing seems certain: the reader in the year 1963 is more likely to see and accept the ambiguity than was the reader in the second year of the Great Depression. He may also perceive a further complication: that Savott's views on mergers and evolution relate closely to his daughter's views on the divine creative mind, and that Savott's general attitude toward life is like Evelyn's. In the course of his argument, Savott says, " all I know is I feel in my bones I've got to go *on* "; in the last paragraph of the book Evelyn thinks of himself, " he knew merely that he was going straight on."

The justification for the luxury world of the Imperial Palace rests with Evelyn's conception of himself and his employees as priests and nuns; or it rests with Gracie's notion of God's infinite presence; or it rests with Savott's quasi-religious, evolutionary economics. These answers imply that for Bennett the Imperial Palace is more than a hotel; it is a microcosm that bears comparison with the great world. What is the justification for the latter? The criticism that Geoffrey West makes of Bennett's luxury world represents Bennett's own philosophical outlook upon the macrocosm: " The entire thing . . . is dedicated to the service of a vulgar, competitive, unproductive, sexual existence; there is scarcely one person in it who serves a really *necessary* need."

Bennett describes his characters as little gods. Of Evelyn, he writes: " He lived his life by deep impulses into which he never inquired. He rather despised individuals who were always worrying themselves about themselves. His attitude was God's: I am that I am." Of Savott at the conclusion of negotiations for the merger, he writes: " Mind alone is creative. Sir Henry Savott had now all but thought his Merger into existence. One more touch, and the vast design would magically appear, visible. . . ." Of Evelyn and Gracie together at the opera in Paris, he writes: " Individuality ceased; he was not he, Gracie was not she; nobody in the audience was anybody. All were merged into a single impersonal, shining, shimmering integrity of primal mind. Evolution had reversed, and at an incredible speed swung

back through eons into the causal eternity before the Word
moved upon the waters and before even the waters were. . . ."
These quotations call to mind some basic themes of all
of Bennett's novels; the last calls to mind especially the
themes of *The Glimpse*. Here as in the earlier novel Bennett is preoccupied with appearance and reality, with isolation and union. (Note the terms " merger " and " merge "
in the second and third quotations; through them Bennett
binds his material together.) These themes embrace fundamental problems of human existence, that existence which
is a gift, a luxury—of God or of evolution, as one wishes—
but still a luxury, rejected by few.

    And yet West's judgment is absolute. There is in the
end no answer to his indifference to Gracie. No more than
there is an answer to the judgment that Christopher Newman is a bore, that Kate Croy and her " great " friends are
bores. If literature is to be regarded as something more
than a wonderful hollow structure ingeniously sustained
in mid-air, this sort of reaction must be acknowledged as
legitimate. Works that have survived the centuries seem
to be those toward whose characters we respond deeply,
sympathizing with them, admiring them. *Pride and Prejudice* is a well-made novel, its machinery delightfully efficient;
but we return to it for Darcy and Elizabeth; we would not
be so pleased were Wickham and Lydia the chief cogs in
the machine. It is perhaps apparent, though, that West's
response might have been different had he thought that
Imperial Palace was written two hundred years earlier. And
it is possible, given the rapprochement of our cultural
community with capitalism in the past decade, that an
audience today is more prepared than West was to read the
novel compassionately and dispassionately. Its justification
may not need to be logical. The reader may respond to
the energy of the novel, to its joy of life. He may withhold

a moral judgment upon Gracie and see her as she is: a beautiful and passionate animal, a twentieth-century version of that lively and passionate eighteenth-century girl, Sophia Western. He need not like Gracie more than Sophia.

It is, to begin with, a masterfully written novel. Bennett's longest work by some forty thousand words, his most complex in plot and action, it is handled with complete authority. Even those critics who have disliked the work have usually acknowledged that it is the product of a highly skilled craftsman. A close examination of its characterization will display subtlety, sophistication, and coherence comparable to those of his other major novels.

The hotel itself dominates the scene—in a certain respect. Its history, organization, and character are described. Built in mid-Victorian times, it was, as the "Royal Palace," a unique achievement:

> In the late 'fifties the Palace luxury had made it the wonder of the earth. It was then reputed to have a bathroom on every floor; and some people stayed in it in order to see what a bathroom was really like.

Then in 1876, when Victoria became Empress of India, the owner changed the name to "Imperial Palace." Its subsequent history has been uneven, and now its royal suites, "owing to a dearth of royalty, were . . . occupied by cinema-kings, presidents of republics, and similar highnesses." But the hotel remembers its history:

> In the lounge were two cloak-room attendants, knee-breeched and gorgeous, who looked as if they had escaped from the Court of the Prince Regent. . . .

It will not do to take such a hotel seriously unless one is a character in the novel. Or will it? Evelyn and Gracie go for a walk on a rainy night, and see the hotel from a distance:

They had come out on the top of the Duke of York's Steps, into the full force of the south-west rain-bearing wind. Not a soul on the Steps. Automobiles flitting in both directions along the Mall below them. Lamps on both sides of the Mall obscured at moments by the swishing branches of trees. Beyond, the dark forest of St. James's Park, with a gleam of the lake. And beyond the forest, high in the invisible firmament, the flood-lit tower of the Imperial Palace poking itself brilliantly up to the skies. There was nothing in all London, then, but that commanding great column of white light.

The hotel is dominated by Evelyn. He is the central figure of the novel. The hotel exists only because he is, as one of the hotel directors says, a "great organizer . . . having a large amount of imagination." When he contemplates his hotel he sees himself as "the creative artist surveying and displaying his creation." No wonder that "the emotional accents of Gracie's rich voice moved Evelyn" when, on the Duke of York's Steps, she calls him a poet. No wonder that he sometimes rises at 4 A. M. He exhibits the kitchen of the hotel to Gracie, the bowels of it to Violet; he is the master of every detail of its operation. He soothes the nerves of his head housekeeper, solves a problem in the Laundry, keeps departmental rivalries at a precise, efficient pitch, makes every guest feel like a king or queen. Should he not, then, feel like a little god? "His attitude was God's: I am that I am."

Gracie thrills to him. At the outset of the novel she sees this masterful man: "'Ah!' she reflected with a yearning. 'His instinct for handling people! Could he handle me? Could he handle me?'" When Evelyn first sees Gracie, he thinks, like a proper artist: "Work first, career first, women second, even were she another Helen." He is tempted, but his temptation is a brief interlude in his life, a couple of days out of twenty years. Not many artists have done better. Of course he masters her; he voyages to Cythera. And still he thinks of her as an artist would. " What a mind! What breasts! " he says to himself. But after he masters her, she rejects him. He realizes then, as the reader has known, that he did not master her, that " she had seduced him."

Gracie invites him into her hotel apartment in Paris. He sits in the drawing room and reads. She goes into the bedroom and gets into bed; she calls to him, and he comes. " 'I think I must have some tea,' she murmured, eyes directed toward the ceiling." He gets her some tea. She confesses that she loves him but urges him not to respond, not to say what he feels until the next day. They talk. She is wearing pyjamas, and when she leans forward " he could not fail to see her sumptuous breasts." He boldly kisses her. They talk. They have supper served in the apartment. She chases around in her night clothes. Finally he says, " I shall have to be off soon."

" But surely, darling," she murmured, facing him with a candid, artless look of pure amazement. " Surely you aren't thinking of leaving me here all by myself to-night." Her eyes moistened.

The masterful man stays, and travels through her to Cythera. But then he must leave for London. She sends after him a note rejecting him. He is offended. His thoughts become savage. He thinks, " What I ought to do is to go back with a cane and rip everything off, and give her a hiding until she fainted away." He does not realize that Gracie would very likely enjoy the hiding. He remains in London. He turns his attention back to the hotel and to Violet Powler, who has neither Gracie's mind nor her breasts.

Evelyn is a trifle absurd. Engaging, yes. Clever, yes.

Handworking, yes. But absurd. He never recognizes the fact. When Gracie rejects him he calls himself a rogue and peasant slave; he is dramatizing rather than condemning himself. He possesses that blithe (sometimes savage) vanity that all of Bennett's characters possess. See him in the opening pages of the novel as he watches Gracie's maid going to the elevator. He reflects that "every nervous movement and glance of the girl divulged her station." (The girl is contemplating suicide.) See him a little later waiting twenty minutes for Gracie, who has promised not to delay him: "During the second ten minutes he grew resentful. It was just like these millionaires to assume that nothing really mattered except their own convenience." (Gracie is tending her servant's wound.) See him later discovering a spot of blood on Gracie's frock and explaining why she got it on her frock instead of her cloak while they were at Smithfield Market. ("What a detective you are!" is all that Gracie says.) He observes that she begins to blush, and he thinks: "How sensitive she was! No doubt she hated the thought of blood on her frock." (Gracie has handled the bloody suicide attempt with composure, and then gone off with him to Smithfield's, where she has had pleasant fantasies of bathing in Smithfield blood.) Not until several pages later does the reader himself learn of the maid's suicide attempt. He has an opportunity then to reflect upon the naïveté of Evelyn's reflections. Bennett does not remind him to. Evelyn goes on spinning his insights throughout the novel. Omniscient he is, like a little god or a little child.

Yet Evelyn remains an attractive figure. By virtue of being the person from whose standpoint the reader sees most of the action, he gains some sympathy. His pride and vanity are understandable. He is manifestly a decent person. If he manages to blur moral issues on occasion (as with the newspaper story on the Caractacus), he nevertheless possesses genuine moral fiber—like Sophia Baines, even though she steals money from her aunt. What is most attractive about him is his joy in his hotel. As Gracie says, "You're a perfect child with a toy!" He is glad to rise at 4 A. M.; he is pleased to know all the complex operations of the organization; he almost never wearies of meeting the crises that arise. He is not like Prince Hamlet; he is, as regards the hotel, a man of abounding energy and very happy in the exercise of it. Surely one can say he and his hotel are absurd. Surely a child and his toy are absurd. Bennett conveys both his absurdity and his attractiveness.

But Gracie, who has sumptuous breasts, is more attractive. She is, perhaps, Bennett's most impressive female character, certainly his most complex. In an early *Journal* entry, written just after he completed his first novel, Bennett notes a conversation with a friend, Alexander Webster, about women in fiction:

> I convinced him and myself that no serious attempt has yet been made by a man to present essential femininity; also that the chasm between male and female was infinitely wider and deeper than we commonly realized. . . .

A good portion of Bennett's career was devoted to trying to present essential femininity. *Anna of the Five Towns, Leonora, Sacred and Profane Love, The Old Wives' Tale, Hilda Lessways*, and two fine short stories, "Elsie and the Child" and "The Woman Who Stole Everything," all focus upon women; and such novels as *The Pretty Lady* and *Riceyman Steps* give close attention to the analysis of female character. (Three of Bennett's lighter novels, incidentally, have women as the main characters.) Gracie comes near the end of a long line; and she represents the fullness of Bennett's understanding as well as the sureness of his skill in portrayal. The portions of *Imperial Palace* that concern her and Evelyn are the best of the book.

The course of her actions in the novel forms a counterpoint with Evelyn's. Near the beginning of the novel, Evelyn shows her the kitchen of the Imperial Palace. She is overwhelmed. " ' I must work! ' she exclaimed, in a rich, passionate whisper. ' I must *work*! This place makes me ashamed. I wish I could put a pinafore on, and work here. . . .' " But as she displays herself in the rest of the novel she is mainly " idle . . . , materially useless to society." She wants desperately to work, but at the end of the novel she is merely pregnant. Evelyn, on the other hand, when he first sees Gracie, is " starved of women " and attempts to indulge his frivolous sensual appetite. But he cannot escape his need to work. At the end of the novel he has solved his sexual problem by marrying; but he gives his devotion to his work. In another way, Gracie and Evelyn are very much alike: they are preoccupied, respectively, with the sensual and material aspects of life. Gracie reads Eddington and writes a book, but she is mainly an animal. Evelyn keeps all sorts of information in his head and organizes complex operations, but he is basically a child with a toy. They possess in their ways a joy of life, sensual and material.

Gracie has considerable if not infinite variety. She is a reckless girl: she is a professional automobile racer; on board ship she was " the only woman at dinner " at the height of the storm that split the ship, and later she " put her little foot into the split." Such an attitude accounts for her inviting herself to go to Smithfield's Market at 4 A. M. with a man she has known for six minutes. It accounts for her violent sensations there, where she is the sole girl in a " world of males " and blood: " With satisfaction she imagined the free imaginings behind their eyes." But as she says to Evelyn (" like an imploring child ") in inveigling

him into taking her, "I'd be as small as a mouse." She
impresses the honest meat buyer, Cradock, by her "honest
manner."

Her recklessness enables her to invade another male sanctuary, the cocktail bar of the Palace, which is reserved for
men. Here, though, she is the serenely poised woman, conscious that her beauty will justify her every act: "a young
woman, a beautiful woman, proud of bearing, clad in a
magnificient frock of mauve and pink, and glinting with
jewels. And neither apology nor challenge in her mien."
She says sweetly to Evelyn and Sir Henry, "I got tired of
waiting for you in the foyer," and she asks Evelyn whether
he thinks a pub would be more up-to-date than his bar.
(She has recently taken Evelyn, for the first time in his life,
into a London pub.) She leads the two men off to the
dining room, where they have supper and watch a dance
by a female entertainer, who virtually does what Gracie
wanted to do before Evelyn at Smithfield's. Gracie "tried
to strip her mind to him, tear off every rag of decency,
expose it to him, nude." Now, after the indecent dance,
she is transformed from the elegant, self-contained woman
in the cocktail bar into an honest and passionate girl.
Evelyn and Savott dissemble their feelings (Savott makes
a judicious comment about the artistic quality of the performance), but Gracie says, "It was shameless," and then
when Evelyn protests, says, "I loved it for being shameless. . . . Why shouldn't it be shameless? . . . What's the
matter with the flesh anyway? Don't we all know what we
are?" A few minutes later, while Sir Henry is away from
the table, she invites Evelyn to dance with her. "In the
middle of dinner?" he asks, and refuses. When Sir Henry
returns, Gracie says, "'Mr. Orcham and I are going to have
just one dance, daddy. . . . You get on with your trout.'"
On the dance floor she seems to Evelyn to be innocent,
devotional.

Then there is the philosophical Gracie, no less passionate, no less innocent, explaining to Evelyn a book on mental science, explaining it with an " eager, radiant face."

" And what's Troward's line? " Evelyn asked, carefully serious to suit her new mood.

" God's his line," she answered, with a sort of fierceness. The divine creative mind. That's his line. If the divine creative mind is infinite, we are *it*. You and me, and all those people there. And these chairs and the lights from the chandelier. Everything. No getting away from it.

She is not an abstract philosopher. She lives according to her views. With her characteristic straightforwardness she explains to Evelyn in Paris why she abandoned him at the Palace and why she called him up again in Paris:

" The walk in the rain [in London, when she calls him a poet] was lovely, and we *were* near—weren't we?—only somehow things were very chilly, very chilly. But when we met at Calais like that, I thought that couldn't be just accident. I don't believe in chance, but I do believe in providence —God. Yes, I do. I believe God's in everything. . . . So I rang you up.

She explains her female intentions toward Evelyn and other men in the same terms. Having said once that he is a poet, she tells Evelyn in Paris, when he is in the toils of her embrace, that women are the enemies of art:

It's their nature, and so it's right, because the divine mind did it. . . . It's God himself, working out his plan. . . . And when she's clasping him tight, and he struggles, and he gives up struggling and the artist in him sighs terribly and dies happy in her inflexible arms, and she smiles, that's God's smile. It's a tremendous moment.

She tells Evelyn of a man, Leo Cheddar, who has been her victim:

Wherever I go he goes. He's quarrelled with his brother because of me. His character is as splendid as his mind. But I couldn't love him. I tell you I could kneel down and crouch on my breasts before him, and wash his feet with my tears, and absolutely implore him to forgive me. But he knows there's nothing to forgive. He knows it's no more my fault than it's his.

Gracie, as her philosophy suggests, is most impressive in the bedroom. Having enticed Evelyn there (" ' I think I must have some tea,' she murmured, eyes directed toward the ceiling "), she holds him with feminine variety. She can be a helpless, desolated child that he must protect; or she can be a mother to hm: " Now, you comic child, sit up and drink some tea. . . . Wait a moment. He must have his mummy's dressing gown over his shoulders." Or she can have a childish tantrum, or she can be a tigress. She is beautiful every moment of it. Evelyn comes upon her in her bath:

She lay in the steaming bath, white and pale pink, idly splashing: amphibious; a marvelous, shameless, indecorous vision.

Gracie is an animal. Three times she says to Evelyn, " I'm a beast." She adds, " But I'm honest." She is a woman Evelyn does well not to marry. For, as she says, she would devour him. He lacks masterfulness, and so returns to his hotel. And Gracie crouches on her breasts before the man she does not love, Leo Cheddar, and marries him.

The joy of life that Gracie and Evelyn possess sustains *Imperial Palace*. If the reader thinks that Gracie is merely a tramp and that Evelyn is merely a fool, then there is no joy. Walter Allen calls the novel " an epic of dullness." But at least one may acknowledge the sort of philosophical detachment that sees their joy. In a short story written

many years before, "The Matador of the Five Towns,"
Bennett expresses his viewpoint through his narrator, a
cosmopolite who makes an examination of the Five Towns:

> I enjoyed all this. All this seemed to me to be fine, to throw
> off the true, fine, romantic savor of life. I would have altered
> nothing in it. Mean, harsh, ugly, squalid, crude, barbaric,—
> yes, but what an intoxicating sense in it of the organized
> vitality of a vast community unconscious of itself!

The narrator can afford to say this, since he is going back
to London. There is some irony intended. But Bennett
himself, after he had got out of the district at the age of
twenty-one, was able to come back and record in his *Journal*
not merely his "shudder" at the sight of the district but
also "the romance of our fight against nature . . . , the
immense secular struggle for existence." The narrator
speaks for him. Both are, fortunately, detached. Years later
when Bennett sat at the New Year's Eve dinner at the Savoy,
he lacked detachment in observing "the noisiest, vulgarest,
costliest thing of the sort I ever had anything to do with."
He went away and gained detachment. If the crude and
barbaric life of the Five Towns can intoxicate one, then
the crude and barbaric life of London can. The abiding
merit of *Imperial Palace* is that it throws off the true, fine,
romantic savor of life. It is a comic novel.

CHAPTER 8

Conclusion

IT IS A long way from realism to romanticism. When Bennett's critics say that he describes the romance of the commonplace, they mean that he tries to make the prosaic interesting. They do not close a gap. It is a long way from Bursley to Xanadu; it is almost as far to Tintern Abbey. No one who travels the distance can fail to be impressed by it. Historically, of course, the journey is not from Bursley, but to Bursley. And what interests the literary historian is not merely the distance but also the route. Is there any other road to Bursley except from Xanadu? And once the route is known, does the distance seem as immense as before?

The prior task is to locate Xanadu, to define the elusive term romanticism. That task cannot be undertaken here. But if (as M. H. Abrams argues in *The Mirror and the Lamp*) the romantic revolution was not one of the minor turns of the wheel that occur every fifty or hundred years or so in literary history but an event that upset views sanctioned for two thousand years, the difficulty in defining romanticism may stem from the fact that its boundaries of influence have not yet been measured. In a certain respect, as Abrams points out, the romantic (expressive) theory of poetry, which swept away the Greek notion that art is imitation, was itself quickly superseded by the modern (objective) theory, which sees the art work neither as an expression nor as an imitation but as an independent organism, a heterocosm. Outside of the poetic stream, though, a mode of art arose—realistic fiction—that is commonly supposed to have readopted the Greek viewpoint with a vengeance. Here is the artist holding the mirror or the camera up to nature; he is self-effacing, impartial, not even attempting to improve nature, restraining the impulse to inscribe a moral under his picture. This is the conventional description of Bennett at his best; it is the common view of the realistic writer. It puts him at a far remove from the romantic poet and also from the modern. For the objectivity of the realist is thought to be much different from the new objectivity. The realist's created world stands in a one-to-one relationship to the real world; it aims to be the real world, even though it cannot be; whereas the modern poet's world is a world unto itself, created by an artist who acts as a reagent, a catalyst (T. S. Eliot's platinum wire in " Tradition and the Individual Talent ") , developing something new and strange. In this fundamental way, the realistic novelist seems to stand with the classical poet and against the romantic and the modern. Xanadu seems to have been bypassed. Yet, as has been shown, Bennett describes his art in romantic terms.

Here is on one hand the romantic hero asking a rhetorical question: "Are not the mountains, waves, and skies a part/Of me and of my soul, as I of them? " Here is on the other hand the realistic hero exclaiming about his bourgeois wife: " What a romance she has made of my life! " Here is the natural man versus the urban man, the large-minded man versus the small-minded, the rebel and individualist versus the hapless conformist, the passionate man versus the petty, the lover of freedom versus the lover of comfort, the anguished soul versus the anxious. To be sure, Childe Harold seems to some of Byron's readers as intolerable a bore as Edwin Clayhanger in *These Twain* seems to some of Bennett's. (Don Juan, who is capable of puking, is at once a better and more realistic hero.)   Nevertheless, the distance between the two is great.   Yet Bennett asks of his hero the same question that Byron puts into his hero's mouth: Are not a child, a horse, a whip, and a canal a part of him and of his soul, as he of them?   And with Bennett the question is not rhetorical.   He describes the creative relationship between mind and external reality, describes the petty world of Edwin's eye and ear—both what they half create, and what perceive.   Burslem is within two hundred miles of both Tintern and Newstead Abbies.

At the outset of his career, Bennett wrote, " The day of my enthusiasm for ' realism,' for ' naturalism,' has passed." He has been shown to be a psychological portraitist of considerable penetration; he has been shown to be a sophisticated and systematic symbolist.   Later in his career he wrote, " No novelist has yet, or ever will come within a hundred million miles of life itself. . . . The convention chosen by an artist is his illusion of the truth."   He has been shown to be an allegorist, creating illusions—perhaps they should be called heterocosms—that bear not a one-to-one but a distant relationship to reality.   Again at mid-career he wrote, " in the sense meant by the average critic, I am not photographic," and elsewhere he described his art in Wordsworthian terms: " all literature is the expression of feeling, of passion, of emotion . . ."; " the book is nothing but the man trying to talk to you, trying to impart to you some of his feelings."   His basic feelings, it has been shown, are those of amusement and compassion in response to the human situation; his tone of voice is manifest in his prose style.   At no time beyond the first couple of years of his career did he concede to realism anything more than technical usefulness in attaining his romantic end: " My desire," he said, is to depict the deeper beauty while abiding

by the envelope of facts." He has been shown in his creation of mournful, grave, sensuous images—"variations on
the theme of beauty."

This display of his art offers problems for the literary
historian. It is not only the problem of a close connection
with the romantics but also the problem of an immediate
connection with the French, Russian, and English novelists
from whom he learned his craft and alongside of whom
he practiced it. The nature of the so-called realist tradition,
the elements of its heritage from the past, and the relationships among the writers who figure in it are problems that
will vex the historian for years to come. And the answers
will affect and be affected by another problem: that of the
relationship of the realists to the novelists since the first
World War, those who seemingly dispossessed the realists
and those who appear to be their legitimate heirs. As was
pointed out in the Introduction, the first group owes an
unquestionable debt. The debt of the second group is
questionable, since such writers as John Wain and John
Braine have many more books to write. The problem that
besets the definition of realism may be the same as that
which besets the definition of romanticism: the boundaries
of its influence have not yet been measured. It is an interesting fact that John Wain comes from the Five Towns.

When all is said and done, Bennett remains a realist in
the most serious sense. The epitaph that he wanted for his
grave was not " he tried to create illusions," but " he tried
to destroy illusions." Although he thought that he was a
million miles from life, he did not turn his back on it.
" The notion that art is first and the rest of the universe
nowhere," he wrote in *The Author's Craft*, " is bound to
lead to preciosity and futility in art." Art for art's sake,
which is one of the bases for the modern conception of the

art work as a heterocosm, was attractive to Bennett, as some comments in his *Journal* make clear; but he kept the rest of the universe in mind. No one would argue that the less dedicated the artist, the better his art. There is, as Bennett knew as well as Yeats or Joyce, a choice that the artist must make for art over life; and Bennett's life was dedicated mainly to art. But he did believe that devotion could lead to a dead end. In the early sixties it does not seem as philistinic as it once did to ask how sharply the artist ought to turn away from life, to ask whether he can afford to devote himself almost entirely to a wonderful heterocosm ingeniously sustained in mid-air. Not many people, scholars or not, read *The Old Wives' Tale* today. Still fewer, it would appear, read *Finnegans Wake*.

The most serious sense in which Bennett remains a realist is the most ordinary sense. His art is a vulgar art; it is intended for ordinary people; it aims to speak of life in a manner comprehensible to them. The title of Book Four of *The Old Wives' Tale* need not be perplexing. For all the necessary ingenuity of construction, for all the sophistication of characterization and theme that lies hidden from casual eyes, the book speaks directly to the ordinary intelligence. So does that touching moment in *Clayhanger*, when Big James, upon learning that Darius has had a stroke and may die, says to Edwin, " But for over twenty years I've worked for him, and now he's gone, never will I lift my voice in song again! " The moment is prepared for three hundred pages in advance when Big James sings proudly and powerfully at the " Free and Easy "; it has ironies that are worth exploring; and it is bound intricately to the basic image of the novel. But it is most impressive in an immediate ordinary way.

There may be some justification, then, in concluding this study of Bennett's art by offering an opinion on it by

an ordinary person. I will call him Orgreave. He was a
pottery manufacturer in Burslem who was recommended
to me as a person who knew something about the Bennett
family. We talked for several minutes about Bennett as a
man. Then he said: " The people here don't like him. But
they don't know him; they don't read him. They only know
that he left the Potteries and didn't come back and said
some nasty things about it. But they don't read him. I
can't get my son to read him. And my daughter asks me
what she ought to read after *The Old Wives' Tale*.

" But I'll tell you something. I gave an old potter a
copy of *The Card* when he retired. The man hadn't read
a book before he was fifty, but he devoured that book and
bought every Bennett book he could lay his hands on. And
you know why? Because Bennett had us between covers."

I said, " A couple of people I've talked to have said that
Bennett didn't know the Potteries."

He said, "Who were they? They weren't natives."

" They were younger people."

" No. It's all there. And with just the right touch. Bennett never gilded the lily, and he didn't understate. Do you
understand what I mean? "

I said, " How do you mean it? "

He replied, " I will tell you a story. Three years ago my
mother died. She was an old woman who had lived all her
life in the Potteries. One night I was sitting by her bed.
She was dying, and she knew she was dying. I was sitting
there reading *These Twain* to myself." He pointed to a
window shelf where numerous papers and a book lay in a
heap. " There it is, right there," he said, and he went to
the window and got the book. " My mother said to me,
' What are you reading? ' She couldn't read any more; she
was blind. I told her. She said, ' Read to me. Read me
the chapter about the funeral.' "

Orgreave said to me, "You remember when Auntie Hamps dies. . . ."

"Yes," I said.

"So I read it to her." He said to me, "Let me read it to you."

I nodded, and he opened the book and read. I realized afterward that Bennett had drawn the description from the death of his own mother.

In the drawing-room the coffin with its hideous brass plate and handles lay upon two chairs, and was covered with white wreaths. At the head of the coffin was placed a small table with a white cloth; on the cloth a large inlaid box (in which Auntie Hamps had kept odd photographs), and on the box a black book. The drawn blinds created a beautiful soft silvery gloom which solemnized everything and made even the clumsy carving on the coffin seem like the finest antique work. The three ministers ranged themselves round the small table; the others stood in an irregular horseshoe about the coffin, nervous, constrained, and in dread of catching each other's glances. Mr. Higginbotham, by virtue of his age, began to read the service, and Auntie Hamps became "she," "her," and "our sister"—nameless. In the dining-room she had been the paragon of all excellences,—in the drawing-room, packed securely and neatly in the coffin, she was a sinner snatched from the consequences of sin by a miracle of divine sacrifice. . . .

Then Orgreave looked up from his reading and said, "When I finished the passage my mother turned and whispered to me, 'Yes, that's just the way it was.'"

The Supposed Unevenness
of Bennett's Work

THERE ARE THREE related evaluative positions taken individually or together by almost all of Bennett's critics: that his Five Towns novels are generally superior to his other work, that he and his art declined after *The Old Wives' Tale* or *Clayhanger*, and that there is a sharp and clear distinction between the good and bad novels. W. Somerset Maugham's view on the first point is succinct: " He never knew anything intimately but the life of the Five Towns . . . and it was only when he dealt with them that his work had character." " Intimately," " life," and " character " are the key terms. They are pleasantly abstract. How does one measure the degree of intimacy with which a diffident youth viewed life in a small section of Burslem, or the degree with which a diffident adult viewed life in small sections of London, Fontainebleau, and Paris? One suspects, though, that Bennett's domineering father, a man who would not let his children go out of doors in the evenings to see what the Five Towns were like, succeeded for a long time in preventing anything but familial intimacy. At any rate, the boy who left the Five Towns when he was twenty-one and never returned save for short visits was not yet the man who understood the minds of Sophia Baines and Edwin Clayhanger.

The testimony of Bennett's associates, including Maugham (who around 1904 were not expecting any significant

work from him) , and the evidence of his art suggest that a
raw youth developed into a mature man. Had Bennett
possessed in 1889 the technique to write *The Old Wives'
Tale* he surely would have lacked the knowledge of people
to give it the substance it possesses. He wrote to George
Sturt in 1904: "Life is a devilish odd thing. I think I
have learnt more about it during the last three years than I
ever knew before." A *Journal* entry of April 1, 1908, reads,
"I expect I am as happy now as I can be. I have learnt a
lot, and am learning." In 1920 Bennett wrote to George
Moore: "It was the first chapters of *A Mummer's Wife*
which opened my eyes to the romantic nature of the district
that I had blindly inhabited for over twenty years." Even
if one allows for the moment that Bennett's Five Towns
novels are his best, he apparently learned about the minds
of the people whom he put into those novels while he was
in London and France. He conceived *The Old Wives' Tale*
while he was looking at an old woman in a Paris restaurant.

There is another irony. The only novel other than the
Five Towns novels to receive nearly unanimous acclaim
from the critics is the one novel that concerns a world
Bennett did not know at all. *Riceyman Steps* should lack
"character." Its bookshop setting derives from an accidental visit by Bennett to a bookshop in Southampton.
He returned to the shop a few times, talked with its pro-
prietor, and purchased there a book by F. S. Merryweather,
Lives and Anecdotes of Misers, from which he drew a little
material for the novel. The scene against which he portrays
the shop is Clerkenwell, a district of London with which
Frank Swinnerton says he was unfamiliar. And the two
major characters of the novel do not, so far as is known,
derive from people known to him personally. For contrast,
consider *The Pretty Lady* and *Lord Raingo*. Bennett had
had a mistress for some time; he had had prolonged experi-

ence during the war on civilian committees and in govern-
ment service. These two war novels with their prostitute-
heroines should possess more "character" than *Riceyman
Steps*—even though they might possess little. Maugham's
view is unsatisfactory. Bennett himself took another view.
At a time when he was just finishing with his Five Towns
novels and was preparing to turn toward modern London,
he said, "When the real intimate work of creation has to
be done—and it has to be done on every page—the novelist
can only look within for effective aid."

In support of the opinion that Bennett and his art
declined after *The Old Wives' Tale* or *Clayhanger*, Bennett
himself is sometimes quoted. According to Marguerite
Bennett, he said on the day of publication of *The Old
Wives' Tale*, "I shall never be able to do better." The
charge is made from several standpoints: (1) he wrote for
money and preoccupied himself with material self-aggrand-
izement; (2) the war killed his spirit; (3) the postwar
world left him behind with prewar notions; (4) during the
war he became primarily a journalist and thereafter gave
too much of his time to journalism; (5) he cut himself off
from his roots in the Five Towns and ceased to write about
them; (6) he came to possess less and less of a private life,
more and more of a superficial public one; (7) he gradually
lost his mental powers; (8) he consumed himself with his
death wish. These views can be responded to in order.

(1) There is no evidence from Bennett himself that any
of his fiction and drama composed after *Buried Alive* (which
he wrote while he was also writing *The Old Wives' Tale*)
was written with a purely or even primarily commercial
end in view. Reginald Pound brackets several novels of
later years as "rent-paying novels," including among them
The Pretty Lady. Geoffrey West quotes *The Truth about
an Author* (published in 1903) to support his contention

that Bennett wrote fiction and drama with money as the main end in view all his life. Walter Allen says of the late novels *The Vanguard* and *Accident* that " they were conceived as commercial articles. . . ." Pound and Allen do not offer evidence to support their opinions. The evidence that West adduces concerns *Teresa of Watling Street*, which was written during or before 1903.

Bennett clearly and admittedly wrote fiction and drama after 1907 of varying quality; but for him the basis of distinction was not " serious " versus " potboiling " but " serious " versus " light." Some writing, he declared in a letter to Sturt, was " the damnedest nerve-shattering experience "; the composition of *Clayhanger*, he noted in the *Journal*, drove him " nearly . . . mad." Other writing he regarded as a " lark "—as his friend Pauline Smith, the novelist, put it. She travelled with him during the time he wrote two light works, *The Card* and *The Honeymoon*. Dorothy Cheston Bennett, who looked askance at light novels such as *Lilian* and *The Vanguard*, found her husband defending them. He thought that *Lilian* would not please the public because the heroine pays no visible price for her sexual sins. He wrote to Dorothy of *The Vanguard*: " I must say that I can see nothing whatever against my writing things like *The Vanguard* quite apart I mean from finance. I *will not* always be writing grave and gloomy plays." (He was at this time working on his play *The Return Journey*.) In the *Journal* Bennett wrote of *The Pretty Lady* that it along with *Riceyman Steps* was " jolly well constructed," and he wrote of *Accident* while composing it, " It seemed to me to be sound and interesting; of course, old fashioned—at least I suppose so." That *The Pretty Lady* is well constructed has been suggested in Chapter Six; that it is serious has probably been adequately proved. In any case, the only novel after *Buried Alive* about which there is any hint by Bennett that commercialism bore some large share in its being written was *The Card*—which by most critics is considered to be one of his four best works. The fact that in his first ten years as a writer Bennett wrote frequently for money and was then able to come up with *The Old Wives' Tale* is worth noting. He commented in his *Journal* on the sensational stories of the early work *The Loot of Cities,* " I have learnt a lot about the technique of construction while writing them." He thought that *Buried Alive* was " a really honest work." It is. And it is better than *The Card.*

(2) The war shocked Bennett, just as it shocked D. H. Lawrence; but there is no evidence that it crippled his spirit. So far as artistic productivity is concerned, his most prolific period was 1904-10; his next most prolific period appears to have been 1925-30, with the years 1911-15 about equal. See Appendix B. Among the 1904-10 productions are three novels, two of them collaborations, and three plays, all of them collaborations, mainly or wholly written as commercial vehicles. Measuring esthetic achievement in terms of productivity is hazardous—even if one wishes to measure one inversely to the other. Certainly Bennett's mind was highly active in late years as in early. Its greatest measurable test came near the end of his career with *Imperial Palace,* his longest work, in detail and setting requiring of him the greatest efforts of memory and organization, and in the structure of its action the most complex. There is no doubt, either, that in complexity of metaphor, imagery, characterization, and theme, Bennett's major novels after the war are generally more impressive than, say, *The Old Wives' Tale.* Admittedly the word " spirit " means nothing so measurable as memory, power, and cleverness. The problem must be left at this: there is no substantial evidence of Bennett's spiritual death at the time of the war.

(3) The charge that the postwar world left Bennett behind is made most seriously by Virginia Woolf, who in her essay claims that human nature changed around 1910 and that Bennett failed to see the change. Later in her essay she says that " Mrs. Brown is eternal, Mrs. Brown is human nature, Mrs. Brown changes only on the surface. . . ." Percy Lubbock, who in other respects admires Bennett, expresses disappointment that such a work as *Mr. Prohack* evades (seemingly) the great changes that the war has wrought upon English society; and Edmund Wilson remarks wryly on the publication of a novel about a luxury hotel in the second year of the depression. Bennett might have replied to these critics that he wrote of what he knew or thought he could know and that as an artist he was (like Virginia Woolf) in search of human nature under the cover of social crisis or calm. He did write two war novels which were serious studies of modern men and women, and in *Imperial Palace* he did explore modern economic problems. His modern girl, Gracie Savott, who knows all about her body and feels desperate about her soul, makes Mrs. Woolf's modern girl, Lily Briscoe, who is interested in woman's rights and a painting career, seem very old-fashioned indeed. Gracie belongs in the company of Myra Viveash and Lady Brett.

(4) Bennett's war service as a journalist and his later journalism to support two women and some personal luxury consumed much time and energy. But the period of 1925-30 was second only to that of 1904-10 in creative productivity, and his art increased in complexity with the years. Nor are the fruits of the years 1916-19 and 1922-23 negligible.

(5) Bennett admittedly cut himself off from his roots. He did so in 1889 when he went to London, in 1903 when he went to France, and again when he ceased to write about

the Five Towns except in a rare short story. The metaphor cannot be used with any consistency to explain his artistic successes and failures. The broader implications of the matter have been discussed in Chapter Seven and also immediately above.

(6) With the favorable reception of *The Old Wives' Tale*, Bennett came into the public light and remained there. He was seen where he had not been seen before. That he attended first nights was not by preference, according to him: he was a playwright and knew many theatre people to whom he felt social and personal obligations. In any event, such public appearances and activities did not preclude a daily life that was mainly private, more private than most people's lives. He gave three hours a day to what he described to Dorothy as "a very delicate, complicated, and exhausting business"; and he gave several more hours to reflection upon his next day's work and to other esthetic and intellectual activities: piano-playing, painting, and reading. (He was a very capable pianist, a fairly accomplished water-colorist, and an omnivorous reader.) That he chose in the evening to go to the theatre, to go to concerts, to see people, does not seem culpable.

(7) W. J. Turner has remarked that *The Return Journey* (1928) showed that Bennett's mind had ceased to think, if it ever had begun to think. Bennett displayed no talent for metaphysics, none for theoretical physics, either when he wrote *How to Live on Twenty-Four Hours a Day* or when he wrote "Einstein for the Tired." But his intellectually most sophisticated non-fictional work, *The Religious Interregnum*, came in 1929. His most complex novel came in the same year.

(8) Grant that Bennett was possessed of a strong death-wish. It is far from certain that such an urge should ad-

versely influence his art. According to one view, all artists
are abnormal people; according to another, normality itself
is a fiction. It can be argued that anyone's death-wish might
contribute to rather than detract from his capacities for
organization and synthesis. At any rate, Pound's depiction
of Bennett draining his life away in the struggle to produce
Imperial Palace is the picture of Bennett producing most
of his serious novels all his life. As his longest and most
complex work, *Imperial Palace* must have demanded the
greatest effort from him, but characteristically he became
ill in writing his books and was sometimes driven to bed
upon their completion. Some persons other than Pound
describe Bennett of the last years as a man with masklike,
weary countenance. Others describe him differently. Herbert Gorman, who saw him in Paris in 1930 with James
Joyce, describes a man who is in excellent humor and who
has clear plans for the future. Bennett suffered all of his life
from dyspepsia and insomnia, he was inclined to diffidence
in public, and he had a customary public pose. Many
people saw a mask. Some saw the man who possessed the
joy of life that *Imperial Palace* evidences.

The third evaluative position taken by Bennett's critics
is that there is a sharp and clear distinction between Bennett's good and bad works. Apart from the unanimous
opinion that *The Old Wives' Tale* and *Clayhanger* are
good and the nearly unanimous opinion that *Sacred and
Profane Love* and *Lilian* are bad, there are serious differences of judgment among the critics. *The Pretty Lady*
affords the most striking illustration. (See the comments on
it quoted in Chapter Six.) It is worth noting that there
is no consistent relationship between Bennett's attitudes
toward his individual works and his critics' opinions of
them. Walter Allen thinks that *Sacred and Profane Love*,
a serious novel for which Bennett had high hopes, "must

be almost the most tasteless novel ever written by a major
novelist." He prefers *The Grand Babylon Hotel*, which
was a potboiler, to *Imperial Palace*. Along with most critics,
he admires *The Card*, which Bennett thought had " no real
distinction."

Bennett's comments on his writing—his letters, journals,
journalism, etc., as well as his novels—are of some use. In
a letter of 1912 to an American woman, Bennett remarks:
" When I contemplate the sheer brains that . . . [George
Meredith] puts into his letters I marvel, but have no desire
to imitate. I have merely a desire to write no letters whatever. When my letters are collected and published—and
nothing that I can do will stop that happening—my posterity
will certainly be disappointed and feel itself aggrieved."
A letter to Dorothy Cheston Bennett of many years later
says, " I can't write long letters like you can. I only want
to say a certain amount, *très simplement*, and then I don't
want to spoil it." There is a good deal of truth in both of
these statements; and yet Bennett wrote well above ten
thousand letters, many of them both long and fine. After
his father's death he wrote every day to his mother; he wrote
weekly letters to his nephew Richard; he wrote regularly
to his literary agents, the Pinker firm. The surviving correspondence to the Pinkers numbers more than two thousand
items; the actual total was probably above three thousand;
one of the letters is two thousand words long. There is also
a large correspondence with literary friends: Gide, Huxley,
George Moore, the Sitwells, George Sturt, Frank Swinnerton, Wells, and many others. With the exception of the
Wells correspondence, most of these letters are unpublished.
Among Bennett's best letters are some of those to Dorothy
Cheston Bennett. The published letters to his nephew omit
the most interesting material of the actual letters. The

letters to Marguerite Bennett remain unpublished except
for a fragment reproduced on the endpapers of *My Arnold
Bennett.*

Bennett's intentions with regard to his journal have been
discussed by George Sturt, whose own journal along with
those of the Goncourt brothers may have inspired Bennett's
decision in 1896 to begin one: "There were to be no
vaporings or rhapsodies; introspection was barred out; spec-
ulations on the riddle of the universe were discountenanced
. . . ." A letter from Bennett to Sturt of June 23, 1896, says
much the same thing and adds that he does not intend the
journal to provide literary material. A letter of 1901 to Sturt
expresses disgust with the journal: "The fact is I am too
ignorant of everything to observe the phenomena with any
fineness. . . . I haven't got down a single thing of any
importance, though naturally I have found some drolleries."
Another letter to Sturt of 1907 remarks that he is still
keeping the journal but does not think it is any good. He
would have agreed with the common criticism that the
Journal is superficial. As late as 1907 he did not think he
was succeeding even in the limited purpose he assigned
to it.

He appears to have regarded his journalism in a similar
light. In a letter to his nephew Richard that echoes remarks
made elsewhere, he mentions his connection with the short-
lived but fine journal, the *Realist*:

> Tonight I'm dining with a group of eminent scientists and
> sociologists . . . apropos of a new monthly that is to be
> started. . . . They want my advice. That is natural. But
> what *isn't* natural is that they want me to write the intro-
> ductory article for the first number. This, my dear sir, is
> summat of a compliment to a mere all-round ignorant
> journalist who has no exact knowledge about anything.

His journalism paid him well, and he generally enjoyed

the work. He wrote toward the end of his life in some private notes quoted by Pound, " I always had a strong feeling for journalism. . . ." In *The Savor of Life* he says: " I have never expressed opinions that I do not hold; nor have I ever been asked to express such opinions." His journalism is characteristically light, humorous, and com-monsensical. Individually, his articles are usually enjoyable; they are the product of a civilized and witty mind; together, as in the several collections of them, they pall upon the reader—as does any anthology of disconnected, light, short, topical pieces. Some of his journalism is dull and foolish. As he says in *The Savor of Life*, " I always write as well as heaven permits."

Special comment is required upon his pocket philosophies, travel books, and a few long essays. In 1907 he wrote to Sturt of his current pocket philosophies: " I see myself now as a sort of moralist for the people. It is a strange role, but I find I am a most serious man, at bottom. . . . At the end of this year I shall have jolly near written 365,000 words . . . much of which is nothing but Marcus Aurelius and Christ assimilated and excreted by me in suitable form." Some twenty years later he wrote in a more serious vein in *The Savor of Life*:

> Many years ago I wrote a series of articles on the daily organization of time for the *Evening News*. They excited considerable interest. When I proposed to republish them in book form I was most strongly urged not to do so, and terrible prophecies were made to me of the sinister conse-quences to my reputation if I did. I republished them. *How to Live on Twenty-Four Hours a Day* sold very well from the start; it still has a steady sale, and it has brought me more letters of appreciation than all of my other books put together. I followed it up with a dozen or more books in a similar vein. And I do not suppose that my reputation

would have been any less dreadful than it is if I had never published a line for plain people about the management of daily experience.

To a sophisticated mind, the pocket philosophies must necessarily seem superficial. Of them all *The Feast of St. Friend,* " my little book on Xmas," is his best; it is warm, humane, commonsensical. It is not philosophy, but it bears reading.

Three of Bennett's travel books, *Paris Nights, From the Log of the Velsa,* and *Mediterranean Scenes* were perhaps conceived at a higher level than most of his journalism, and by their nature they retain more interest. Only on the last of them is there significant comment by Bennett: a *Journal* note that " I have decided the form of my cruise articles, namely the disjointed note form—rather like Taine's *Notes sur l'Angleterre,"* and a comment to Dorothy on " my beautiful *impressions de voyage."* These books contain many fine passages. Among other journalistic pieces, the essays in the privately printed *Things Which Have Interested Me, Third Series,* some of which are reprinted in *Paris Nights,* are uniformly excellent. *The Author's Craft* is an interesting study of Bennett's own craft. *The Religious Interregnum* is a valuable discussion of the decline of religion.

Bennett's early comments on his fiction and drama show him to be uncertain of his talent. In letters to Sturt he writes: " I may say that I have no inward assurance that I could ever do anything more than mediocre viewed strictly as art—very mediocre "; " I know I haven't got the creative impulse necessary for a big thing, but I fancy I can by sheer force of concentration and monotony do something effective in a small way "; " I think I have settled in my own mind that my work will never be better than third-rate, judged by the highest standards, but I shall be cunning enough to make it impose on my contemporaries." A few years later in an exchange of letters with Frank Harris over *The Old Wives' Tale* he speaks confidently of his technical capacity to deal with his plain subjects: " If I cannot take a Pentonville omnibus and show it to be fine, then I am not a fully equipped artist (and I *am*.) " On nearly the same day that he wrote this letter he was writing in an article, " Intimations of Immortality," that it was " incontestable that at the end of the century I shall be dead." There is some humor here and perhaps a well-founded trepidation over the English sales of the just-published *The Old Wives' Tale*. At any rate, from that point on his remarks display confidence in his technical mastery of organization and detail. On the day he finished *The Card* he wrote in the *Journal*: " Stodgy, no real distinction of any sort, but well invented and done up to the knocker, technically, right through." He thought that *The Pretty Lady* and *Riceyman Steps*, as he records in the *Journal*, were " jolly well constructed." He criticized D. H. Lawrence, whom he admired greatly, and Virginia Woolf, whom he admired less, because he thought they were careless in construction. All the same, his final opinion of the significance of technique was that one given in *The Author's Craft*:

> I am obliged to say that, as the years pass, I attach less and less importance to good technique in fiction. I love it, and I have fought for a better recognition of its importance in England, but I now have to admit that the . . . greatest novelists of the world, according to my own standards, have either ignored technique or have failed to understand it. . . . I begin to think that great writers of fiction are by the mysterious nature of their art ordained to be ' amateurs.'

The technical mastery which he has been shown to possess will not save him by his own standards. Looking at his books as artistic wholes, Bennett was more doubtful than not of their merit. His opinion expressed to Dorothy late in life that *Anna Karenina* " is so much superior to any novel I could write " probably reflects considered judgment.

Bennett's plays are usually thought to be much inferior to his novels, and the opinion is common that he wrote many or most of them as ephemeral commercial products. On at least two occasions Bennett noted that beginning with *Cupid and Commonsense*, written in 1907, none of his plays was written except with an artistic end in view. All of his published plays, with the exception of the three one-act plays collected in *Polite Farces*, he considered serious attempts of art. Some of his plays he regarded more highly than some of his serious novels. Bennett thought that his play modelled upon *Anna of The Five Towns*, *Cupid and Commonsense*, was superior in its ending, and he probably thought that it was superior all round: " one of the best things I have ever done," he wrote in the *Journal*. His comments on *Don Juan, Judith,* and *The Bright Island* indicate that he thought highly of them.

In *The Author's Craft*, repeating remarks that he makes elsewhere, Bennett compares play-writing and novel-writing. He calls the playwright " a sub-novelist " and says that play-writing is easier than novel-writing. " On the average," he says, one may say that it takes six plays to make the matter of a novel. Other things being equal, a short work of art presents fewer difficulties than a longer one." He argues that a play cannot afford the sustained subtlety that a novel can; that in scenic and physiognomic description the dramatist has no struggle; that in character portrayal he can and must rely heavily on his actors; that in the most difficult problem of convincingness, of being true to life, the dramatist by the presence of his actors has an easier task—if only to deceive. George Bernard Shaw took offense at Bennett's opinions. He wrote an essay in which he argues that the Bible does not weigh as much as the London Directory but is a better book; and that *Macbeth* is better than a prose paraphrase of it that Bennett might produce.

Lafourcade, who has given more attention to the plays than most of Bennett's critics and who is generally sympathetic to Bennett's work, has little to say in favor of them. He concludes his discussion by remarking that Bennett " never lavished much labor on them. They were mostly written within two or three weeks." His conclusions may be questioned. With the possible exception of *A Man from the North* and *Anna of the Five Towns*, Bennett appears to have given more attention to the revision of his plays *Flora* and *Mr. Prohack* than to any other works. Appendix B shows only three of his non-commercial plays written within three weeks; one of them is known to have been preceded by a preliminary draft. Considering that Bennett could produce the 160,000 words of *Clayhanger* in less than five months, the amount of time he devoted to any work is significant only in the respect that it could be astonishingly little. Although the plays have not received any attention in the present book, they merit serious study. The comedies *What the Public Wants, The Title*, and *The Bright Island* stand comparison with the best of the comic novels; *Judith* is a fine work that brought praise from Thomas Hardy; and *Don Juan* and *The Return Journey*, although uneven, are serious, original dramas of unusual interest.

Bennett was equally emphatic on a couple of occasions that the art of the short story is less difficult than that of the novel. He nevertheless practiced the art seriously, and some of his stories are among his finest works. Two early stories, " The Death of Simon Fuge " and " The Matador of the Five Towns," are frequently singled out for praise.

Bennett himself comments favorably on the former, and he probably thought well of the latter. It seems likely, though, that he would have chosen some of the stories of his later years over them. In the *Journal* he calls " The Cornet Player " " the most original story I've ever written "; he says that " The Woman Who Stole Everything " is " one of the best I had ever done "; and he feels that " Elsie and the Child " is much too good a story to be appearing in the *Storyteller.* Upon " The Wind," which seems to this critic to be one of his very best stories, there is no comment by him available. Some of his other good stories are " Death, Fire, and Life," " The Elixir of Youth," " Middle-Aged," " Nine O'Clock Tomorrow," " One of Their Quarrels," and " The Umbrella." Most of these stories, and the best of them, do not concern the Five Towns.

Bennett as a novelist occupies, in contemporary literary history, the second or third rank—as do the realists generally. In the present study he has been shown to be much more than a realist, and he has been shown to possess many of the qualities that modern critics value. But it is hardly likely that he will be moved forward in the ranks in the near future. Final judgment upon an artist rests on something more profound than critical analysis. Although Virginia Woolf fails to perceive the depths of Bennett's characterizations, fails to grasp his ironical perspective, fails to recognize his coherent imagery and symbolism, fails to discern his disinterested compassion, she may have judged him rightly: he may not have been worth her serious attention.

One of Bennett's own failures may throw light on the problem. *Sacred and Profane Love*, a novel for which Bennett had high hopes, has seemed to most of his critics, including the present writer, to be a highly unsuccessful work. Walter Allen calls it " almost the most tasteless novel

ever written by a major novelist." That it is an artfully
conceived book, artfully executed, subtle in structure and
characterization, equal in these respects to many rightly
esteemed novels, there is no doubt. But some artists, and
some of the best, are notable for occasional lapses of taste;
their art walks a tightrope over absurdities. Perhaps Bennett fails in *Sacred and Profane Love* in the same way that
Wordsworth fails in " Peter Bell." At any rate, he was not
trying to write a tasteful novel; and for the critic to say
that *Sacred and Profane Love* is stylistically ludicrous and
emotionally embarrassing is to miss its intention. Bennett
risked these qualities; he wanted to allow a foolishly romantic woman to disclose herself. In his Preface to the
American edition of the novel, he writes (responding to
the views of some of his women readers) :

> The style of the following pages is not my style; it is the
> style of Carlotta Peel. Nor are the views on art and conduct
> expressed by Carlotta Peel necessarily my views. Nor am I
> minded to defend everything that Carlotta Peel did. But
> when I am asked as I have been asked (with a lift of the
> eyebrows) : " Surely you don't think her a *nice* woman? "
> I emphatically reply: " Yes, I do."

The basic problem in evaluating *Sacred and Profane Love*
is one of sympathy. Bennett asks the reader not to enjoy
the novel stylistically, not to expect emotional heights, not
to admire Carlotta's foolishness of action, passion, or intellect, but to come to a better understanding of a woman
through a sympathetic sharing of her life. If the reader can
set aside prejudices of taste, exercise his capacity for sympathy, think of Carlotta Peel as a nice woman, he may
find *Sacred and Profane Love* to be a modestly good novel.
    Perhaps Bennett asks too much of the reader. Carlotta
Peel may not be worth the effort. Bennett cannot afford to

be foolish in describing foolishness. The reader with a strong sense of taste has a right to be offended. He ought, too, to be offended by the following letter from Robert Schumann to Clara Wieck, which could have been written by Carlotta to the pianist Diaz:

> I have hit upon the following joint plan—I shall play tomorrow, on the stroke of 11, the adagio from Chopin's "Variations," and at the same time I shall concentrate all my thoughts on you. Now please do the same thing, so that we may meet and our spirits mingle.
>
> I am hoping for your answer. If you should not do this, and if a string should snap tomorrow in the twelfth hour— it would be myself. I speak with my whole heart.

Some of Bennett's other novels about romantic people have possessed more taste. Which are his best novels? To single out his best novel is difficult. Perhaps it is *Clayhanger*, perhaps *The Old Wives' Tale*, perhaps *Lord Raingo*. A choice among their excellences does not seem very meaningful. Two things do seem clear: that with *The Old Wives' Tale* Bennett attained a maturity as an artist that he never relinquished, producing during the rest of his life several works of approximately equal merit; and that by and large his London novels are superior to his Five Towns novels. Even if one grants that *Clayhanger* and *The Old Wives' Tale* are Bennett's very best novels, all the other novels that stand close to them in merit are London novels: *Lord Raingo, Riceyman Steps, Imperial Palace,* and *The Pretty Lady.* The weight lies with the second group. (In his *Journal, 1929,* for September 25, Bennett writes, " I have written between seventy and eighty books. But also I have only written four: *The Old Wives' Tale, The Card, Clayhanger,* and *Riceyman Steps.*" On more than one occasion these lines have been offered as

Bennett's own judgment on his writing. In context, they
express his cognizance of a common judgment among his
critics.)

The general superiority of Bennett's London novels,
along with other later works that do not deal with the Five
Towns, is, to this critic, quite clear. All the best plays
(*Judith, What the Public Wants, The Bright Island*, and
Don Juan), all the best short stories (" The Wind," " The
Cornet Player," " Elsie and the Child," " The Woman Who
Stole Everything "), the best comic novel (*Buried Alive*),
the best entertainment (*Accident*), and the only good sen-
sational novel (*The City of Pleasure*) wholly or mainly
concern London or some historical or fanciful setting rather
than the Five Towns. There are, of course, some other
Five Towns works of merit: *These Twain, The Price of
Love, Hilda Lessways, The Card, Cupid and Commonsense,*
and *Anna of the Five Towns.*

Bennett's range of effort is worth noting. His plays are
realistic (*Cupid and Commonsense*), romantic (*Don Juan*),
biblical (*Judith*), comic (*The Great Adventure*). He wrote
one play along the lines of Italian *Commedia dell' arte*
(*The Bright Island*). His novels show great variety: humorous melodrama (*The City of Pleasure*), serious melodrama
(*The Price of Love*), supernaturalism (*The Ghost*), comedy
(*Buried Alive*), tragedy (*Anna of the Five Towns*), family
chronicle (the *Clayhanger* tetralogy), regional novel (those
of the Five Towns), cosmopolitan novel (*Imperial Palace*),
social problem novel (*Whom God Hath Joined*), domestic
novel (*These Twain*), political novel (*Lord Raingo*), first-
person confession (*Sacred and Profane Love*), trilogy of
parallel lives (*Anna of the Five Towns, Leonora, Sacred
and Profane Love*). In these novels Bennett portrays a
variety of human and social types: prostitutes, misers, finan-
ciers, cards, artists, provincials, cosmopolites, servants, aristo-

crats, criminals, bureaucrats. His scenes vary: they may be homely as in *The Old Wives' Tale*, voluptuous as in *Imperial Palace*, dramatic as in *Clayhanger*, comic as in *The Card*, tragic as in *Anna of the Five Towns*, grotesque as in *Riceyman Steps*, pathetic as in *The Pretty Lady*. " Life for me," Bennett wrote in his last years in *The Savor of Life*, " has many savors, which I relish keenly. Therefore many subjects interest me."

APPENDIX B

Gestation and Composition; Chronology of Composition

THE AMOUNT OF attention that Bennett gave to his art is impressive. For several of his novels there is evidence of years of preliminary contemplation. *The Old Wives' Tale* was conceived in November of 1903 and lay germinating in his mind until September of 1907. *Riceyman Steps*, which he began to write toward the end of 1922, emerged from fragments that date as far back as 1907—with his interest in the theme of miserliness going back at least ten years more. *Lord Raingo* appears to have been conceived five years prior to the time of composition, and it draws upon material that dates ten years back. *Imperial Palace* is foreshadowed in *The Grand Babylon Hotel* and *Hugo* of thirty and twenty-five years earlier; numerous fictive and journalistic discussions of hotels over the years imply frequent thought upon the subject before March of 1927, when Bennett decided to write the novel, a date two and a half years prior to the actual writing.

Specific preparation before composition usually consumed considerable time. *The Old Wives' Tale, Clayhanger, Riceyman Steps*, and *Imperial Palace* required months of preliminary research. Bennett says in his Preface to *The Old Wives' Tale* that he did not enjoy research, but for that book, for *Clayhanger*, and for *The Glimpse*, he did research on such matters as the siege of Paris in the Franco-Prussian War, labor conditions in early nineteenth-century England,

and theosophy. For *The Old Wives Tale, Clayhanger,* and *Lord Raingo* he conversed at length with persons who themselves had experienced the events he wished to describe or who had other pertinent information; after the last book was completed he "vetted" its medical and political material with his authorities. For *Clayhanger, Riceyman Steps,* and *Imperial Palace* he revisited scenes once familiar to him and made several tours of unfamiliar realms in order to obtain suggestions of material and information for his descriptions. Much of his writing, however, did not demand such research. Just as *The Old Wives' Tale* was largely written out of his knowledge of Burslem, as he knew it in his youth and as he came to understand it in his maturity, so most of *The Pretty Lady* was written out of his experiences in Paris years before, his committee activities in London during the war, and his knowledge of the crusade against "vice" in the theatres which was conducted by the clergy during the war. It should not be assumed that any of the information gained either through research or through ordinary experience went directly into the substance of the novels. In a preliminary study of the making of the novels, "Some Curious Realism in *Riceyman Steps*" (see the Secondary Bibliography), I have shown that Bennett radically transformed the material that he drew from a history of Clerkenwell and from a book about misers.

Regardless of any necessity for research, many or all of Bennett's novels, serious and light, appear to have been preceded in their composition by a period of active conceptualization. Possessing a mind not only fertile in invention but capable of a large grasp, he could develop his subject rapidly and competently. Three of his comments in the *Journal* on *Clayhanger* show him at such work. November 19, 1909, at Fontainebleau, a month and a half before he began writing the novel and at least two months after he had begun research on it: ". . . in the forest I practically arranged most of the construction of the first part of the novel "; December 8 at Burslem, after he had spent the previous evening at a theatre for a similar purpose: " I had got into an extraordinary vein of ' second sight.' I perceived whole chapters "; January 3, 1910, at Brighton, just before he began writing: " I . . . schemed out the first nine chapters." That the same process was followed with lighter works can be illustrated with *Dream of Destiny*, the novel he left unfinished at the time of his death. In her article in the *Bookman*, Dorothy Cheston Bennett says that he let *Dream of Destiny* gestate in his mind for months before composing it; he knew the whole construction and characterization and had written the plot in short story form—from a somewhat different angle—as " The Dream," a story that appears in the collection *The Night Visitor*. (A similar account is given in a letter by Bennett to Eric Pinker, quoted by Pound.) Bennett wrote to his nephew Richard two months before beginning to write the book, " My next novel is all in my head."

Bennett's preliminary notebooks for his novels were sometimes elaborate. The notebooks for *Imperial Palace* run to more than three hundred pages; those for much shorter works sometimes run to more than a hundred. A preliminary inspection of these notebooks indicates that they are primarily concerned with character, action, and theme of the novel proper; they contain only a small amount of the quarry material of a realistic novelist. Interestingly enough, the material is fragmentary and disordered. It seems to reflect a compulsive gesture in the direction of writing rather than a central activity of conceptualization.

It is hardly to be supposed that the beginning of writing marked the end of conceptualization. The *Journal* records many walks along streets and in forests and visits to art galleries and museums that were Bennett's characteristic strategy for freeing his mind to develop works in progress. But his detailed conceptions enabled him to produce both his serious and light works swiftly. *The Old Wives' Tale* was begun October 8, 1907, was set aside during most of December of that year and all of January and February of 1908, was resumed in the middle of March, and was completed at the end of August. In eight months devoted to the book, Bennett produced 200,000 words. In the two months of January and February, after having written a scenario in December, he wrote his light novel *Buried Alive*, which is about 60,000 words long. It would be impossible to say whether he did the writing of one novel faster than that of the other. In the *Journal* he records writing 1,700 words of *The Old Wives' Tale* in two and a half hours and 4,800 words of *Buried Alive* in a single day.

The speed and sureness with which Bennett wrote are due not only to his grasp upon his subject and to his remarkable energy; they also spring from his general view of his art. In the sense that he lived from the income of his writing, he wrote for money, and wrote *The Old Wives' Tale* as well as *Teresa of Watling Street* for money; he did not curry whimsy in his writing habits. Secondly, he had too modest an opinion of his novels to believe that reliance upon either inspiration or revision could contribute significantly to their worth. Thirdly, his general esthetic views and his opinions on artistic method disinclined him to undertake extensive revision. Fascinated though he was by problems of technique, impressive though his own technique is, he felt that—as he wrote in the *Journal*—the " essential characteristic of the really great novelist . . . is a Christ-like, all-embracing compassion," and that—as he wrote in *How to Become an Author*—" good style is not a bird that can be brought down with a shot-gun."

Despite his opinions, Bennett wrote carefully and on occasion subjected his writing to extensive and prolonged revision. It was not necessarily the best of his work that he revised. His plays *Mr. Prohack* and *Flora* appear to have been among the most radically revised of his manuscripts, the former completely revised once, and its first and third acts revised a second time, Bennett's labors on it covering a three-year period. He remarked on one occasion that plays generally require more revision than novels. Among his novels his first two serious ones, *A Man from the North* and *Anna of the Five Towns*, appear to have undergone much more extensive revision than any of his later novels. In his prefatory note to the facsimile edition of *The Old Wives' Tale*, Bennett remarks, apropos of the beautiful calligraphy which he developed especially for the writing of this novel:

> Of course if your manuscript is to have even the most modest pretensions to calligraphic decency, you must know all the time exactly what you are about to do; otherwise a regular mess will ensue. It will be noticed that now and then in the writing of *The Old Wives' Tale* something rather like a regular mess did ensue, consequence of not having absolutely decided in advance just what I wanted to write, and in what order, and how. The reader, however, sees the worst of these messes; no page, so far as I remember, was destroyed and rewritten. . . .

It is doubtful that very many manuscripts of like scope by other writers bear so few corrections as this one does. Its most impressive passages show no more correction than its more ordinary ones.

That there were other than conscious reasons for Bennett's writing habits—perhaps compulsiveness and rigidity of psyche—seems obvious enough. The question arises: would he have written better had he blotted more? For several years Bennett wrote poetry, from as early as 1894, when he was writing verses for songs by Herbert Sharpe, to as late as 1912, when he was considering publishing some poetry. His rate of composition contrasted strikingly with the seven hundred words of prose that he could produce in an hour. On July 29, 1907, he wrote in the *Journal*, " I spent an hour and a half yesterday morning in writing 4 lines of verse, and another three-quarters of an hour in sketching out 4 more lines. At this rate according to my present spare time, I should accomplish one short poem in about six weeks." He was unsatisfied with the results; according to Pound, he said to a friend, " It's no good—I can't do it."

Two of his published poems were composed just prior to the writing of *The Old Wives' Tale*; and to his detached, self-critical eye they must have offered themselves as evidence that effort and concentration beyond a certain point hindered his creative capacities. In the *Journal* for March 12, 1908, is the following entry:

> I have tried for two days to find rhythms for two poems that I found ideas for—one elegiac and the other Aristophanic, and can't.

> I have read through first part of *Old Wives' Tale*, and am deeply persuaded of its excellence.

Another poem, which Pound quotes in full, " Night on the Riviera," seems superior to the other published poems; but it is derivative, reminiscent of Matthew Arnold's poetry, of which Bennett thought highly, and again could hardly have helped suggesting to Bennett that he bridled his energies without sufficient warrant. He possibly knew the demands, the limitations of his psyche. In " Egotism," written in the 'twenties, he took note of a couple of critical remarks upon his writing habits:

Thus:

> " If he had not so fine an efficiency he might have had a
> talent of the very first quality, if not genius. He has, how-
> ever, modelled himself so well to good craftsmanship in
> writing that one almost gives up hope now of having him
> ever drift into the accident of being a genius."

Again:

> " He is so extraordinarily efficient a writer, that you quite
> despair of him falling into genius, although you often feel
> he could."

These extracts—and I could quote more if my damnable
efficiency would let me—are very precious indeed.

It is worth noting, as an exception to his general failure
in writing poetry, that in 1896 Bennett wrote a fine libretto
to a one-act operetta by his friend James Brown. It is a
slight piece, conceived for performance at a girl's school,
but the rhythms of the verses are impressive. The work
is in the romantic tradition.

Bennett's writing was the chief and consuming activity
of his daily life for all of his mature years. Customarily
he rose early, sometimes as early as five o'clock, to go immediately to his desk to do the important writing for the
day—three hours of work at home, hotel, or on his yacht.
Sometimes in the afternoon or evening he would work on
a light novel or play. An hour or two or more in the afternoon—or in the morning if he had not yet begun a work or
wanted to develop it further—might be devoted to peri-
patetic reflection upon his next day's work. George Doran,
who was a silent companion on many walks at Fontainebleau, said to him once, " I suppose in these silences you
are actually phrasing your thousand words for tomorrow,"
and got " Yes " for an answer.

Despite the suggestion of orderly, efficient labor, most of Bennett's writing was accompanied by physical and mental distress. As was pointed out in Appendix A, some of his writing was " the damnedest nerve-shattering experience." Completing a work was a crisis that frequently drove him to bed. On account of such distress, and also for other reasons, Bennett's daily writing schedule frequently varied and sometimes was abandoned.

In the following chronological table of Bennett's compositions, the variations and minor lapses in his writing schedule could not be taken into consideration. For this reason, if for no other, comparisons of the lengths of time Bennett gave to individual works cannot be significant in estimating his seriousness of intention in writing them. The dates of composition do not include time given to preliminary research or to preliminary drafts. The drafts were sometimes as long as the finished work and often contained much final writing; they have been noted whenever anything about them is known. The dates include subsequent revision only when it is known to have been extensive. By and large, Bennett's first copy was his last copy. The dates of composition are as exact as possible; in some instances information is lacking or vague. The information is drawn mainly from journals, letters, and manuscripts. The word-lengths given are thought generally to be accurate to within about five thousand words; they do serve adequately for comparison. Periodical and serial publications are not listed. The chart includes only the longer and the more important writings.

Year	Title	Time Put into Composition	Word Length	Publication or Production
1893	"A Letter Home" written during year	Unknown	3,500	"A Letter Home" published in *Yellow Book*
1895	*A Man from the North* begun in the middle of April			
1896	*A Man from the North* finished May 15	Less than a year; set aside on occasion	50,000	
1898	*The Ghost* begun about September			*A Man from the North*
1899	*The Ghost* finished January 23	4 months? In *The Truth about an Author* Bennett says he composed it in 24 days. In the *Journal* he says 3 months. A letter to Sturt suggests a longer period. In large part revised during October and November of 1906.	48,990	
	The Gates of Wrath begun during year			
1900	*The Gates of Wrath* presumably finished during year	Unknown	45,000	
	The Chancellor (in collaboration with Arthur Hooley) in composition in February and finished during year	Unknown	4 acts	(*The Chancellor* never published or produced)
	Children of the Mist (in collaboration with E. Phill-	Unknown	4 acts	(*Children of the Mist* never published or produced)

Year	Title	Time Put into Composition	Word Length	Publication or Production
	potts) composed during year and finished by November 14			
1900	*The Grand Babylon Hotel* composed during year	Unknown	55,000	
	Anna of the Five Towns begun during year			
1901	*Anna of the Five Towns* finished May 17	Unknown. Bennett began writing this novel as early as September, 1896. Whether at the time he regarded all of the material he produced in the next 3 years as preliminary is unknown. By March of 1899 he had written 80,000 words of what he then called a draft. The final writing followed.	64,000	
1901 or 1902	*Teresa of Watling Street* begun some time after October, 1900, and completed some time before—probably a considerable time before—October 1, 1903	Unknown	45,000	*The Grand Babylon Hotel*
1902	*Leonora* begun probably toward the end of the year			*Anna of the Five Towns*

Year	Title	Time Put into Composition	Word Length	Publication or Production
About 1902	*Her Grace's Secret* (based on the novel by Violet Tweeddale)	Unknown	4 acts	(*Her Grace's Secret* never published or produced)
1903	*Leonora* finished probably by June 30	4 months or less, mainly written between April and June	65,000	*Leonora*
	The Loot of Cities begun about latter part of September and finished November 27	2 weeks or less; remainder of time given to preliminary work and other writing	31,000	*The Gates of Wrath*
	A Great Man begun about December 10			
1904	*A Great Man* finished March 13	2 months, work interrupted for five weeks	55,000	*A Great Man*
	Christina (probably the same play as *A Credit to Human Nature*, referred to in *Journal*; in collaboration with E. Phillpotts) begun about January 20 and finished February 5 with later revisions	2 weeks or so	full-length play	(*Christina* never published or produced)
	Hugo begun April 19 and finished July 16	Slightly under 3 months	50,000	*Teresa of Watling Street*
	An Angel Unawares (in collaboration with E. Phillpotts) begun about November 1			

YEAR	TITLE	TIME PUT INTO COMPOSITION	WORD LENGTH	PUBLICATION OR PRODUCTION
1904	*Sacred and Profane Love* (novel) begun about November 24			
1905	*An Angel Unawares* finished January 3	2 months or less	full-length play	(*An Angel Unawares* never published or produced)
	Sacred and Profane Love (novel) finished July 16	5 months, interrupted for other work	60,000	*Sacred and Profane Love*
	Que Faire? begun on March 9 and finished on March 18 (intended collaboration with Henry D. Davray)	10 days	2 acts	(*Que Faire?* never published or produced)
	The City of Pleasure begun about April 1 and finished May 30	2 months	60,000	*The Loot of Cities*
	Whom God Hath Joined begun November 8			
1906	*Whom God Hath Joined* finished probably early in July	Somewhat under 7 months, interrupted for *The Sinews of War*	70,000	*Whom God Hath Joined*
	The Sinews of War (in collaboration with E. Phillpotts) begun January 26 and finished April 7	Slightly over 2 months	80,000	*The Sinews of War*
				Hugo

Year	Title	Time Put into Composition	Word Length	Publication or Production
1907	"The Death of Simon Fuge"	Unknown	18,000	"The Death of Simon Fuge" published in *The Grim Smile of the Five Towns*
	Helen with the High Hand probably begun during year and finished by June 15. Bennett wrote a supplementary instalment of 5,000 words on March 28 and 29, 1908.	Presumably two months or less	55,000	
	The Statue (in collaboration with E. Phillpotts) probably begun during year and finished before October 31	Unknown	75,000	*The Ghost*
	Cupid and Commonsense begun August 13 and finished August 29	17 days, preceded by preliminary draft	4 acts	*The City of Pleasure*
	The Sole Survivors (in collaboration with E. Phillpotts) begun September 11 and finished October 4, Phillpotts having done earlier draft	Under a month	3 acts	(*The Sole Survivors* never published or produced)
	The Old Wives' Tale begun October 8			

Year	Title	Time Put into Composition	Word Length	Publication or Production
1908	The Old Wives' Tale finished August 30	8 months, interrupted for *Buried Alive*	200,000	*The Old Wives' Tale*
	Buried Alive begun January 1 and finished February 27	2 months	45,000	*Buried Alive*
	"The Matador of the Five Towns" written during year	Unknown	9,000	
				The Statue
	What the Public Wants begun November 3 and finished December 3	1 month	4 acts	*Cupid and Commonsense* produced
1909	The Card begun January 3 and finished March 1	2 months	65,000	*What the Public Wants* published and produced
	The Glimpse begun May 20 and finished by about August 15	3 months	70,000	*The Glimpse*
	The Honeymoon begun October 5 and finished probably in early December	A month and a half or so	3 acts	*Cupid and Commonsense* published
1910	Clayhanger begun January 5 and finished June 23	Slightly under 5 months, interrupted between each book	160,000	*Clayhanger*
	The Great Adventure begun about October 1 and finished November 11	About a month and a half	4 acts	*Helen with the High Hand*

YEAR	TITLE	WORD LENGTH	TIME PUT INTO COMPOSITION	PUBLICATION OR PRODUCTION
1911	*Hilda Lessways* begun January 5 and finished June 13	100,000	About 5 months	*Hilda Lessways*
	Milestones (in collaboration with E. Knoblock) begun August 1 and finished August 24	3 acts	3 weeks	*The Card*
				The Honeymoon published and produced
				The Great Adventure produced
1912	*The Regent* begun February 14 and finished April 11	80,000	2 months	"The Matador of the Five Towns" published in collection of same name
	The Price of Love begun November 4			*Milestones* published and produced
1913	*The Price of Love* finished September 29	105,000	Probably 8 months or less, interruption of at least 3 months indicated in *Journal*	*The Great Adventure* published
	Don Juan begun December 12			*The Regent*
1914	*Don Juan* finished January 25	4 acts	A month and a half	*The Price of Love*
	These Twain begun about June 1			
1915	*These Twain* finished March 5	145,000	10 months or less	*These Twain*

Year	Title	Time Put into Composition	Word Length	Publication or Production
1915	The Lion's Share begun April 2 and finished December 1	3 months and a half, interrupted from May to September	100,000	
1916	Sacred and Profane Love (play) begun April 13 and finished July 16. (Instinct referred to in Journal appears to be same play)	3 months or less	3 acts	The Lion's Share
	The Roll-Call begun October 16			
1917	The Roll-Call finished April 30	6 months or less	110,000	
	The Pretty Lady begun May 24			
1918	The Pretty Lady finished January 28	8 months or less	80,000	The Pretty Lady
	The Title begun March 24 and finished May 8	A month and a half	3 acts	The Title published and produced
				The Roll-Call
1919	Judith begun January 5 and finished January 27	3 weeks	3 acts	Judith published and produced
	Body and Soul begun July 3			Sacred and Profane Love (play) published and produced

Year	Title	Time Put into Composition	Word Length	Publication or Production
1920	*Body and Soul* finished some time before May 10	Unknown	4 acts	
	The Bright Island begun in the middle of January and finished April 18	3 months or less, some revision in 1923	3 acts	
	The Love Match begun July 1 and finished July 31	1 month	5 scenes	
	Mr. Prohack (novel) begun October 11			
1921	*Mr. Prohack* finished June 16	6 months or less, interrupted for 2 months	105,000	
	The Wedding Dress (film story) probably begun in April and finished April 17	Probably under a month, rewritten from version of previous year	Probably about 18,000	(*The Wedding Dress* never published, uncertain whether produced)
	Lilian begun December 4			*Body and Soul* published
1922	*Lilian* finished January 24	A month and a half	33,000	*Lilian*
	London Life (in collaboration with E. Knoblock) begun about June 1 and finished at end of month	1 month	3 acts	*Body and Soul* produced
	Riceyman Steps begun October 10			*The Love Match* published and produced
				Mr. Prohack (novel)

Year	Title	Time Put into Composition	Word Length	Publication or Production
1923	*Riceyman Steps* finished March 17	5 months	95,000	*Riceyman Steps*
				Don Juan published (never produced)
1924	"Elsie and the Child" begun January 15 and finished February 14	1 month	20,000	"Elsie and the Child" published in collection of same name
	Judith (opera libretto, begun August 16 and finished August 17	2 days	1 act	*The Bright Island* published
	Mr. Prohack (play, in collaboration with E. Knoblock) in composition in August			*London Life* published and produced
1925	*Mr. Prohack* finished January 27	Unknown. Bennett began writing the play as early as June, 1923, finished one version in December of 1924, revised it. Further revision as late as October, 1927.	3 acts	*The Bright Island* produced
	Flora begun about March 4 and finished March 31	Under a month; an earlier version was written in previous year	3 acts	
	Lord Raingo begun May 13			
	"The Cornet Player" begun September 10 and finished September 13	4 days	5,000	

Year	Title	Time Put into Composition	Word Length	Publication or Production
1926	Lord Raingo finished January 26	7 months	140,000	Lord Raingo
	The Vanguard begun February 8 and finished July 8	Less than 5 months, interrupted during trip, considerable rewriting during this time	65,000	
	"The Woman Who Stole Everything" begun July 20 and finished August 11	3 weeks	22,000	
	Accident begun November 26			
1927	Accident finished July 19	6 months or less, interrupted for almost 2 months	70,000	Mr. Prohack (play) published and produced
	"The Wind" begun October 2 and finished October 28	27 days	6,500	The Vanguard
				"The Woman Who Stole Everything" published in collection of same name
				Flora produced
1928	The Return Journey begun February 7 and finished June 21	4 and a half months, revision in July	Prologue and 3 acts	The Return Journey produced (never published)
	Piccadilly (film story) begun May 11 and finished May 24	14 days	18,000	

YEAR	TITLE	TIME PUT INTO COMPOSITION	WORD LENGTH	PUBLICATION OR PRODUCTION
1928	*Punch and Judy* (film story) begun November 12 and finished December 17	1 month	probably about 18,000	(*Punch and Judy* never published, uncertain whether produced)
1929	Untitled play begun January 30 and finished June 13	4 months or less	full-length play	(Untitled play never published or produced)
	Venus Rising from the Sea begun April 24 and finished May 14	3 weeks	24,000	*Judith* (opera) published and produced
	Imperial Palace begun September 25			*Piccadilly* published and produced
				Accident
1930	*Imperial Palace* finished July 5	9 months	243,000	*Imperial Palace*
	Don Juan (opera libretto) begun September 20 and finished October 3	2 weeks	full-length opera	
	Dream of Destiny begun November 25 and left off December 26	1 month	30,000	
1931				"The Cornet Player" and "The Wind" published in the collection *The Night Visitor*
				Venus Rising from the Sea
1932				*Dream of Destiny*
1933				*Flora* published
1937				*Don Juan* (opera) produced (never published)

APPENDIX C

PRIMARY BIBLIOGRAPHY

FIRST PUBLICATION IS listed, whether it occurs in England or the United States. When English and American publication come in the same year, only English publication is listed. Serial publication is not listed. Alternate titles, including serial titles, are given.

NOVELS

Accident, London, Cassell, 1929.

Anna of the Five Towns, London, Chatto and Windus, 1902.

The Book of Carlotta, New York, Doran, 1917; the American title for the novel *Sacred and Profane Love*; contains preface by Bennett not in original English edition.

Buried Alive, London, Chapman and Hall, 1908.

The Card, London, Methuen, 1911.

The City of Pleasure, London, Chatto and Windus, 1907.

Clayhanger, London, Methuen, 1910.

The Deeds of Denry the Audacious, New York, Dutton, 1910; an advance edition, for copyright purposes, of *Denry the Audacious*—as *The Card* was titled in America; the edition consists of the first three chapters of the novel.

Denry the Audacious, the American title for *The Card* (see above).

Doubloons, the American title for *The Sinews of War* (see below).

Dream of Destiny, London, Cassell, 1932; with *Venus Rising from the Sea* (see below).

For Love and Life, serial title for *The Ghost* (see below).

The Gates of Wrath, London, Chatto and Windus, 1903.

The Ghost, London, Chatto and Windus, 1907.

The Glimpse, London, Chapman and Hall, 1909.

The Grand Babylon Hotel, London, Chatto and Windus, 1902.

A Great Man, London, Chatto and Windus, 1904.

Helen with the High Hand, London, Chapman and Hall, 1910. (One copy of the first edition exists in which every page is headed with " Helen of the High Hand "; the copy lacks its covers.)

Hilda Lessways, London, Methuen, 1911.

Hugo, London, Chatto and Windus, 1906.

Imperial Palace, London, Cassell, 1930.

Leonora, London, Chatto and Windus, 1903.

Lilian, London, Cassell, 1922.

The Lion's Share, London, Cassell, 1916.

Lord Raingo, London, Cassell, 1926.

A Man from the North, London, Lane, 1898.

The Miser's Niece, serial title for *Helen with the High Hand* (see above).

Mr. Prohack, London, Methuen, 1922.

The Old Adam, the American title for *The Regent* (see below).

The Old Wives' Tale, London, Chapman and Hall, 1908; later English and American editions contain a preface by Bennett.

The Old Wives' Tale, London, Benn, and New York, Doran, 1927; facsimile of the original manuscript, with a prefatory note by Bennett.

Piccadilly, London, Readers Library, 1929.

The Pretty Lady, London, Cassell, 1918.

The Price of Love, London, Methuen, 1914.

The Regent, London, Methuen, 1913.

Riceyman Steps, London, Cassell, 1923.

The Roll-Call, London, Hutchinson, 1918.

Sacred and Profane Love, London, Chatto and Windus, 1905.

The Sinews of War (with E. Phillpotts), London, Laurie, 1906.

The Statue (with E. Phillpotts), London, Cassell, 1908.

The Strange Vanguard, the English title for *The Vanguard* (see below).

224   *Appendix C*

Stroke of Luck, the American title for *Venus Rising from the Sea* (see below).

Teresa of Watling Street, London, Chatto and Windus, 1904.

These Twain, New York, Doran, 1915.

T. Racksole and Daughter, an alternate American title for *The Grand Babylon Hotel* (see above).

Train de Luxe, serial title for *Accident* (see above).

The Vanguard, New York, Doran, 1927.

Venus Rising from the Sea, London, Cassell, 1931.

Whom God Hath Joined, London, Nutt, 1906.

PLAYS

Body and Soul, New York, Doran, 1921.	Produced 1922
The Bright Island, London, Golden Cockerel, 1924.	Produced 1925
Cupid and Commonsense, London, Palmer, 1909, with a preface by Bennett.	Produced 1908
Don Juan, London, Laurie, 1923, with a preface by Bennett.	Never produced
Flora, published in *Five Three-Act Plays*, London, Rich and Cowan, 1933.	Produced 1927
The Great Adventure, London, Methuen, 1913.	Produced 1911
The Honeymoon, London, Methuen, 1911.	Produced 1911
Judith, London, Chatto and Windus, 1919.	Produced 1919
London Life (with E. Knoblock), London, Chatto and Windus, 1924.	Produced 1924
The Love Match, London, Chatto and Windus, 1922.	Produced 1922
Milestones (with E. Knoblock), London, Methuen, 1912.	Produced 1912

Mr. Prohack (with E. Knoblock), London, Chatto and Windus, 1927.	Produced 1927
Polite Farces (includes 3 plays of one act: *A Good Woman, A Question of Sex,* and *The Stepmother*), London, Lamley, 1900 (published November, 1899).	Only *A Good Woman* produced — under title *Rivals for Rosamund,* 1914
The Return Journey (never published).	Produced 1928
Sacred and Profane Love, London, Chatto and Windus, 1919.	Produced 1919
The Title, London, Chatto and Windus, 1918.	Produced 1918
What the Public Wants, London, Duckworth, 1909.	Produced 1909

COLLECTIONS OF NOVELS AND PLAYS

The Arnold Bennett Omnibus Book (contains *Riceyman Steps,* " Elsie and the Child," *Lord Raingo,* and *Accident*), London, Cassell, 1931.

The Clayhanger Family (contains *Clayhanger, Hilda Lessways,* and *These Twain*), London, Methuen, 1925.

Milestones, The Great Adventure, London, Methuen, 1926 (Methuen's Modern Classics).

The Minerva Edition of the Works of Arnold Bennett, London, Library Press [1926], 7 vols. (*Anna of the Five Towns, Teresa of Watling Street, A Great Man, Whom God Hath Joined, Buried Alive, The Card, The Regent*).

Three Plays (*The Bright Island, Cupid and Commonsense, Sacred and Profane Love*), London, Chatto and Windus, 1926.

SHORT STORY COLLECTIONS

The contents of these collections sometimes vary slightly from edition to edition. The same story may appear in more than one collection.

Elsie and the Child, London, Cassell, 1924.

The Grim Smile of the Five Towns, London, Chapman and Hall, 1907 (contains " The Death of Simon Fuge ").

The Loot of Cities (six related short stories), London, Rivers, 1905.

The Matador of the Five Towns, London, Methuen, 1912 (contains along with the title story and others " The Death of Simon Fuge ").

The Night Visitor, London, Cassell, 1931 (contains " The Cornet Player " and " The Wind ").

Selected Tales, London, Harrap, 1928.

Tales of the Five Towns, London, Chatto and Windus, 1905 (contains " A Letter Home ").

The Woman Who Stole Everything, London, Cassell, 1927.

OPERA AND FILM

Don Juan (opera; music by E. Goosens; never published).	Produced 1937
Faust (film titles by Bennett).	Produced 1926
Judith (opera; music by E. Goosens), London, Chester, 1929.	Produced 1929
Piccadilly (film), London, Readers Library, 1929.	Produced 1929
Rosalys (operetta; music by J. Brown), printed in the appendix of Locherbie-Goff, *La Jeunesse d'Arnold Bennett* (see below, Secondary Bibliography).	Produced 1898

POETRY

" A Love Affair," *Journal*, August 2, 1907.

" Night on the Riviera," Pound, *Arnold Bennett*, pp. 151-52, and in *T. P.'s Weekly* of unknown date.

Rosalys, printed in the appendix of Locherbie-Goff, *La Jeunesse d'Arnold Bennett* (see below, Secondary Bibliography).

" Town and Country," *Journal*, August 28, 1907, and *English Review*, Vol. 3 (October 1909), p. 377.

LITERARY CRITICISM

The Author's Craft, London, Hodder and Stoughton, 1914.

Books and Persons, London, Chatto and Windus, 1917.

Fame and Fiction, London, Richards, 1901.

How to Become an Author, London, Pearson, 1903.

Journalism for Women, London and New York, Lane, 1898.

Literary Taste, London, New Age, 1909.

The Storyteller's Craft, serial title for *The Author's Craft* (see above).

The Truth about an Author, Westminster, Constable, 1903.

POCKET PHILOSOPHIES

The Feast of St. Friend, London, Hodder and Stoughton, 1911.

Friendship and Happiness, a later title for *The Feast of St. Friend* (see above).

How to Live, New York, Sun Dial, n. d. (contains *How to Live on Twenty-Four Hours a Day*, *The Human Machine*, *Mental Efficiency*, and *Self and Self-Management*).

How to Live on Twenty-Four Hours a Day, London, New Age, 1908.

How to Make the Best of Life, London, Hodder and Stoughton, 1923.

The Human Machine, London, New Age, 1908.

Marriage: The Plain Man and His Wife, a later title for *The Plain Man and His Wife* (see below).

Married Life, an alternate American title for *The Plain Man and His Wife* (see below).

Mental Efficiency, New York, Doran, 1911 (the same as *The Reasonable Life* [see below] with some additions).

The Plain Man and His Wife, London, Hodder and Stoughton, 1913.

The Reasonable Life, London, Fifield, 1907.

Self and Self-Management, London, Hodder and Stoughton, 1918.

ESSAY COLLECTIONS

The Savour of Life, London, Cassell, 1928.

Selected Essays, London, Harrap, 1926.

Things That Have Interested Me [First Series], London, Chatto
and Windus, 1921.

Things That Have Interested Me, Second Series, London, Chatto
and Windus, 1923.

Things That Have Interested Me, Third Series, London, Chatto
and Windus, 1926.

Things Which Have Interested Me, Third Series, Burslem, privately printed, 1908.

ART

Bennett, Mrs. Arnold (Marguerite), *Arnold Bennett,* London,
Philpot, 1925, with two water colors by Bennett.

The Book of Carlotta, New York, Doran, 1917, with a water color
by Bennett on the dustjacket.

" A Feudal Town in France," *Country Life,* December 19, 1908,
pp. 885-87, written and illustrated with four pencil sketches
by Bennett.

From the Log of the Velsa, New York, Century, 1914, with a
water color by Bennett.

Ionides, Cyril, and Atkins, J. B., *A Floating Home,* London,
Chatto and Windus, 1918, with eight water colors by Bennett.

The Journals of Arnold Bennett, 3 vols., London, Cassell, 1932-33,
Vol. 2 with four sketches by Bennett (Volume 2 of the 3-
volume edition published by Viking Press in New York has
the same sketches).

(A few of Bennett's water colors and sketches are owned by the
Victoria and Albert Museum, London; other sketches are
owned by the Stoke-on-Trent Museum. See the *Catalogue of
Modern Drawings and Pictures,* below, Secondary Bibliography.)

AUTOBIOGRAPHY

The Truth about an Author, Westminster, Constable, 1903 (published anonymously).

JOURNALS

Journal, 1929, London, Cassell, 1930.

Journal of Things New and Old, the American title for *Journal, 1929.*

The Journals of Arnold Bennett, 3 vols., London, Cassell, 1932-33.

Things That Interested Me [First Series], Burslem, privately printed, 1906.

Things Which Have Interested Me, Second Series, Burslem, privately printed, 1907.

(See also the items from the *Bookman, Life and Letters*, and *T. P.'s Weekly* [see below, miscellaneous Uncollected Writings])

LETTERS

Arnold Bennett's Letters to His Nephew, New York and London, Harper, 1935.

Bennett, Dorothy Cheston, *Arnold Bennett, A Portrait Done at Home, together with 170 Letters from A. B.*, New York, Kendall and Sharp, 1935.

Wilson, Harris, ed., *Arnold Bennett and H. G. Wells: The Record of a Personal and Literary Friendship*, Urbana, University of Illinois, 1959.

TRAVELS

From the Log of the Velsa, New York, Century, 1914.

Mediterranean Scenes, London, Cassell, 1928.

Over There, London, Methuen, 1915.

Paris Nights, London, Hodder and Stoughton, 1913.

Those United States, London, Secker, 1912.

Your United States, New York and London, Harper, 1912 (negligible differences between this and *Those United States* [see above]).

MISCELLANEOUS PAMPHLETS AND OTHER WRITING

The Arnold Bennett Calendar, London, Palmer, 1911.

A Century of Books for Bibliophiles, privately printed [1892 (?)].

A Century of Books for Bibliophiles (a second catalogue), privately printed [1892 (?)].

Frank Swinnerton: Appreciations (with H. G. Wells), New York, Doran, n. d. (also issued by Doran under titles *Frank Swin-*

nerton: *Critical Appreciations* and *Frank Swinnerton, Personal Sketches,* with one or more contributors in addition
to Bennett and Wells) .

How Are You?, privately printed [1928 (?)].

Hugh Walpole: Appreciations (with Joseph Conrad and Joseph
Hergesheimer) , New York, Doran, n. d.

Liberty!, London, Hodder and Stoughton, 1914.

Marcel Proust, An English Tribute (with Joseph Conrad and
others) , London, Chatto and Windus, 1923.

My Religion (with Hugh Walpole and others) , London, Hutchinson, 1925.

A National Responsibility, Future Employment of the Disabled,
Manchester and London, Heywood [1917 (?)].

Our Women, London, Cassell, 1920.

The Religious Interregnum, London, Benn, 1929.

Thoughts on National Kitchens, London, 1918.

Wounded, London, The Wounded Allies' Relief Committee, 1915.

The Wounded Allies' Relief Committee, London, The Wounded
Allies' Relief Committee, 1915.

INTRODUCTIONS

The Art of E. A. Rickards, London, Technical Journals, 1920.

Audoux, Marguerite, *Marie-Claire,* London, Hodder and Stoughton, 1911.

Catalogue of Exhibition of French Art, 1914-1919, London, Man-
sard Gallery, August 1919.

Coward, Noel, *Plays, First Series,* Garden City, New York, Doubleday, Doran, 1928.

Drinkwater, John, *Abraham Lincoln,* Boston and New York,
Houghton, Mifflin, 1919.

Gide, André, *Dostoevsky,* London, Dent, 1925.

Low, David, *Lloyd George and Company,* London, Allen and
Unwin, n. d.

More, Adelyne (C. K. Ogden) , *Fecundity Versus Civilization,*
London, Allen and Unwin, 1916.

Nichols, G. H. F. (Quex) , *London Town,* London, Partridge,
1926.

Phillpotts, Eden, *Widecombe Fair,* The Widecombe Edition of the Dartmoor Novels, Vol. 1, London, Macmillan, 1927.

Playfair, Nigel, *The Story of the Lyric Theatre, Hammersmith,* London, Chatto and Windus, 1925.

Roshner, Harold, *In the Royal Naval Air Service,* London, Chatto and Windus, 1916 (published in America as *With the Flying Squadron,* New York, Macmillan, 1916).

Smith, Pauline, *The Little Karoo,* London, Cape, 1925.

Stopes, Marie Carmichael, *Wise Parenthood,* London, Fifield, 1918.

Sturt, George, *A Small Boy in the Sixties,* Cambridge, Cambridge University, 1927.

Sullivan, Herbert, and Flower, Newman, *Sir Arthur Sullivan,* New York, Doran, 1927.

Vados (Agnes Farley), *The Belmont Book,* New York, Dutton, n. d.

Void of War, An Exhibition of Pictures by Lieut. Paul Nash, London, Leicester Galleries, 1918.

Wadsworth, Edward, *The Black Country,* London, Ovid, 1920.

Miscellaneous Uncollected Writings of Some Importance

" Florentine Journal," *Bookman* (New York), Vol. 66 (November 1927), pp. 244-53, and Vol. 66 (December 1927), pp. 429-38.

" From a French Journal," *Life and Letters,* Vol. 2 (January 1929), pp. 16-28, and Vol. 2 (February 1929), pp. 98-113.

" How I Was Educated," *John O'London's Weekly,* Vol. 23 (June 28, 1930), p. 398.

" A Novelist's Log-Book," *T. P.'s Weekly,* November 13, 1903, to May 6, 1904.

" The Progress of the Novel," *Realist,* Vol. 1 (April 1929), pp. 3-11.

" What Is a Good Novel," *Highway,* Vol. 16 (Summer 1924), pp. 101-102.

" Who I Am," *Daily Express,* June 6, 1928 (one of a series by writers).

" Would I Live My Life Again? " *Sunday Express,* March 17, 1929 (one of a series by eminent persons).

WORKS DRAMATIZED OR FILMED BY OTHERS

The Card (American title: *The Promoter*), a film produced by J. Arthur Rank; Alec Guinness as Denry; script by Eric Ambler.	Produced 1952
Helen with the High Hand, a play by Richard Pryce, New York, French, 1914.	Produced 1914
His Double Life (The Great Adventure), a film produced by Paramount; Lilian Gish and Roland Young as Janet Cannot and Ilam Carve; script by Arthur Hopkins and Clara Baranger.	Produced 1933
Holy Matrimony (The Great Adventure), a film produced by Twentieth Century Fox; Gracie Fields and Monte Woolley; script by Nunnally Johnson.	Produced 1943
Riceyman Steps, a play by Michael Morton.	Produced 1926
Sacred and Profane Love, a film produced by Famous Players; Elsie Ferguson and Conrad Nagel as Carlotta and Diaz; script by Julia C. Ivers.	Produced 1921

WORKS WRONGLY ATTRIBUTED TO BENNETT

Despite satisfactory disclaimers by Bennett himself (see Locherbie-Goff, below, Secondary Bibliography, p. 283; see also Lafourcade, below, Secondary Bibliography, p. 31), the second of these works continues to be listed in Bennett bibliographies; it has also been used to argue that from the outset of his career Bennett was preoccupied with success stories.

Ballads of the Briny, London, Gay and R., 1904.
Sidney Yorke's Friend, London, Wells Gardner, 1901.
Stephen Ashton's Dragon, London, Religious Tracts Society, 1896.

MANUSCRIPT HOLDINGS IN LIBRARIES AND MUSEUMS IN THE UNITED
STATES AND ENGLAND

The five important collections are those held by the Arnold
Bennett Museum, Stoke-on-Trent; the C. K. Ogden Library, Uni-
versity College, London; the New York Public Library; the
Sterling Memorial Library, Yale University; and the University
Library, Cambridge University. For a list of holdings at three
of these and at other libraries see Hepburn, James G., " Arnold
Bennett Manuscripts and Rare Books: A List of Holdings,"
English Fiction in Transition, Vol. 1 (Spring-Summer 1958),
pp. 23-29.

SECONDARY BIBLIOGRAPHY

BOOKS, DISSERTATIONS, PAMPHLETS, AND CATALOGUES ON OR RE-
LATING MAINLY TO BENNETT

Allen, Walter, *Arnold Bennett, Denver,* Swallow, 1949.

Arnold Bennett, An Introduction, New York, Doran, n. d.

*Arnold Bennett, The Original Manuscripts of Many of His Short
Stories, Essays, Plays, etc.,* London, Maggs, n. d.

*Autograph Letters of Bernard Shaw . . . , The Original Manu-
script of Arnold Bennett's Anna of the Five Towns, First
Editions and Presentation Copies of Arnold Bennett,* New
York, Anderson Galleries, 1930.

Banerjee, Srikumar, and Nath, C. B., *Complete Study of The
Admirable Crichton, Milestones, The Great Adventure,* Bom-
bay, Shahani, 1930.

Bennett, Dorothy Cheston, *Arnold Bennett, A Portrait Done at
Home,* New York, Kendall and Sharp, 1935.

Bennett, Mrs. Arnold (Marguerite), *Arnold Bennett,* London,
Philpot, 1925.

Bennett, Marguerite, *My Arnold Bennett,* New York, Dutton,
1932.

Buckstead, Richard Chris, " H. G. Wells, Arnold Bennett, John
Galsworthy: Three Novelists in Revolt Against the Middle
Class," Dissertation, State University of Iowa, 1960.

Catalogue of Books from the Library of the Late Arnold Bennett,
London, Myers, March 20, 1932.

Catalogue of Modern Drawings and Pictures, The Property of Capt. F. Guy . . . , the Late Arnold Bennett . . . , London, Sotheby, July 23, 1931.

Catalogue of the Manuscripts and Correspondence of Arnold Bennett, London, Sotheby, May 25, 1936.

Catalogue of the Personal Library of Arnold Bennett, Consisting Primarily of the Works of His English and French Contemporaries, London, Sotheby, July 27, 1931.

Crockett, William M., " Arnold Bennett—1898-1908," Dissertation, University of Chicago, 1955.

Darton, F. J. Harvey, *Arnold Bennett,* New York, Holt, 1915.

Drabert, Emil, *Frauengestalten in Arnold Bennetts Romanen,* Bonner Studien zur Englischen Philologie, Heft 28, Bonn, Hanstein, 1936.

Essays and Reviews by Arnold Bennett, London, Stonehill, 1938.

Follett, Helen Thomas, *et al., Arnold Bennett, Appreciations,* New York, Doran, n. d.

Ford, John, " Bennett Country," City of Stoke-on-Trent, Information Series, No. 5, April, 1960.

Glaymen, Rose E., " Recent Judith Drama and Its Analogues," Dissertation, University of Pennsylvania, 1930.

Grove-White, Barbara Elizabeth, " Bibliography of Part of the Work of Arnold Bennett," submitted to London University, 1962.

Hall, James Winford, " Arnold Bennett: The Mediation between Primitivism and Taste," Dissertation, Cornell University, 1949.

——, *Arnold Bennett: Primitivism and Taste,* Seattle, University of Washington, 1959.

Harris, Frank, *Frank Harris to Arnold Bennett, Fifty-Eight Letters, 1908-10,* Merion Station, Pennsylvania, American Autograph Shop, August 28, 1936.

Hepburn, James G., " The Mind and Art of Arnold Bennett," Dissertation, University of Pennsylvania, 1957.

Jaeschke, Ruth, " Arnold Bennett und Frankreich," Dissertation Breslau, Plischke, 1934.

Johnson, L. G., *Arnold Bennett of the Five Towns,* London, Daniel, 1924.

Kennedy, James G., "Literary Convention and the Realistic Novels of Arnold Bennett," Dissertation, University of Minnesota, 1961.

Lafourcade, Georges, *Arnold Bennett, A Study*, London, Muller, 1939.

Locherbie-Goff, Margaret, *La Jeunesse d'Arnold Bennett*, Avesne-sur-Helpe, Éditions de L'Observateur, 1939.

Massoulard, Elizabeth, *Die Romantischen Elemente in Arnold Bennett*, Bonner Studien zur Englischen Philologie, Heft 34, Bonn, Hanstein, 1938.

The Personal Library of Arnold Bennett, London, Hollings, 1931.

Pound, Reginald, *Arnold Bennett*, New York, Harcourt, Brace, 1953.

Roberts, Thomas John, "The Reputation of Arnold Bennett Over a Half Century," Dissertation, University of Minnesota, 1958.

Roberts, Thomas R., *Arnold Bennett's Five Towns Origins*, Stoke-on-Trent, Libraries, Museums and Information Committee [1961].

Sanna, Vittoria, *Arnold Bennett, E I Romanzi Delle Cinque Citta*, Firenzi, Marzocco, 1953.

Saveson, Marilyn Buehrer, "The Influence of Emile Zola upon the Theory and Practice of Some English Novelists of His Time," Dissertation, Cambridge, 1956.

Simons, J. B., *Arnold Bennett and His Novels*, Oxford, Blackwell, 1936.

Smith, Pauline, *A. B., '. . . A Minor Marginal Note,'* London, Cape, 1933.

Sotheby & Co.'s Sale of the Manuscripts and Correspondence of Arnold Bennett, London, Sotheby, May 25, 1936.

Swinnerton, Frank, *Arnold Bennett*, London, Longmans, Green, 1950.

Tillier, Louis, "Studies in the Sources of Arnold Bennett's Novels," Dissertation, University of Paris, 1949.

Tresidder, Argus John, "Arnold Bennett," Dissertation, Cornell University, 1935.

West, Geoffrey (Geoffrey Wells), *The Problem of Arnold Ben-*

nett, London, Joiner and Steele, 1932.

West, Rebecca, *Arnold Bennett Himself*, New York, Day, 1931.

Woolf, Virginia, *Mr. Bennett and Mrs. Brown*, London, Hogarth, 1928 (first published 1924).

ARTICLES, LITERARY SURVEYS, AND MISCELLANEOUS BIBLIOGRAPHICAL MATERIAL

There is little periodical literature on Bennett of any significance. Only a few literary surveys give more than perfunctory attention to Bennett's art. The list below consists of those items that seem of some interest or worth. Bibliographical material is marked with an asterisk.

*Astor, Lenox, " Bibliographies of Younger Reputations," *Bookman* (New York), Vol. 34 (November 1911), pp. 325-26.

Beach, Joseph Warren, *The Twentieth Century Novel*, New York and London, Appleton-Century-Crofts, 1932.

Beardmore, F. G., miscellaneous articles on Bennett and the Five Towns in the *Sunday Chronicle* in 1929: February 3, February 10, June 23, June 30, December 22, and other dates.

Beardmore, George, " An Arnold Bennett Museum," *John O'London's Weekly*, Vol. 60 (August 17, 1951), p. 491.

Bennett, Dorothy Cheston, " Arnold Bennett's Unfinished Novel," *Bookman* (New York), Vol. 75 (September 1932), pp. 497-500.

Bennett, Marguerite, " Married to a Genius," *Sunday Chronicle*, August 27 through October 15, 1933.

*Bontell, Henry Sherman, " Modern English First Editions. (Enoch) Arnold Bennett, 1867-," *Publishers' Weekly*, Vol. 117 (March 15, 1930), pp. 1596-1600.

*Bronson-Howard, George, " Arnold Bennett as a Melodramatist," *Bookman* (New York), Vol. 42 (October 1915), pp. 147-54.

Byrne, M. St.-Claire, " Arnold Bennett and His Critics," *National Review*, Vol. 96 (May 1931), pp. 702-6.

**Complete Catalogue of the Library of John Quinn*, Vol. I, New York, Anderson Galleries, 1924.

Drew, Elizabeth, *The Modern Novel*, London, Cape, 1926.

Dunkel, Wilbur D., "The Genesis of 'Milestones,'" *College English*, Vol. 13 (April 1952), pp. 375-78.

Dutton, George B., "Arnold Bennett, Showman," *Sewanee Review*, Vol. 34 (January 1925), pp. 64-72.

*Fabes, Gilbert H., *Modern First Editions*, London, Foyle, 1929-32 (three series).

Hepburn, James G., "Manuscript Notes for *Lord Raingo*," *English Fiction in Transition*, Vol. 5, no. 1 (1962), pp. 1-5.

——, "Some Curious Realism in *Riceyman Steps*," *Modern Fiction Studies*, Vol. 8 (Summer 1962), pp. 116-26.

Hunt, Violet, "Arnold Bennett in Paris," *Bookman* (New York), Vol. 75 (August 1932), pp. 345-48.

Laski, Harold, "Arnold Bennett," *Daily Herald*, March 14, 1931.

*Nicholls, Norah, "Arnold Bennett: Some Bibliographical Points," *Bookman* (London), Vol. 80 (May 1931), pp. 128-29.

Priestley, J. B., "Mr. Arnold Bennett," *London Mercury*, Vol. 9 (February 1924), pp. 394-406.

Rahv, Philip, *Image and Idea*, Norfolk, Connecticut, New Directions, 1949.

Roberts, T. J., "Some Forms, A Meaning, Knowledge: Bennett's 'Matador,'" *Graduate Student of English*, Vol. 1 (Summer 1958), pp. 7-15.

Sherman, Stuart P., *On Contemporary Literature*, New York, Holt, 1917. (His essay on Bennett appeared in the *Nation*, Vol. 101 (December 23, 1915), pp. 741-44, and was followed in succeeding issues by responses from other critics.)

Strong, L. A. G., "The Real Bennett," *John O'London's Weekly*, Vol. 34 (March 21, 1936), p. 957.

Tillyard, E. M. W., *The Epic Strain in the English Novel*, London, Chatto and Windus, 1958.

Wain, John, *Preliminary Essays*, London, Macmillan, 1957.

MEMOIRS, BIOGRAPHIES, NOVELS IN WHICH BENNETT FIGURES

Only a few of special interest or worth are listed.

Bennett, Tertia, *Gentleman Dash*, London, Hodder and Stoughton, 1912.

Flower, Sir Newman, *Just As It Happened*, London, Cassell, 1950.

Ford, Ford Madox, *Reminiscences, 1894-1914*, London, Gollancz, 1931.

Green, Anne, *With Much Love*, New York and London, Harper, 1948.

Hales, H. K., *The Autobiography of "The Card,"* London, Sampson, Low, 1936.

Hart-Davis, Rupert, *Hugh Walpole*, New York, Macmillan, 1952.

Lowndes, Mrs. Belloc, *The Merry Wives of Westminster*, London, Macmillan, 1946.

Sinclair, May, *The Belfry (Tasker Jevons: The Real Story)*, New York, Macmillan, 1916. (Jevons is thought to have been modelled upon and does bear some resemblance to Bennett.)

Sitwell, Sir Osbert, *Laughter in the Next Room*, Boston, Little, Brown, 1948.

——, *Noble Essences*, Boston, Little, Brown, 1950.

Swinnerton, Frank, *Background with Chorus*, New York, Farrar, Strauss and Cudahy, 1956.

——, *The Bookman's London*, London, Wingate, 1951.

——, *The Georgian Scene*, New York, Farrar & Rinehart, 1934.

——, *Swinnerton, An Autobiography*, Garden City, New York, Doubleday, Doran, 1936.

——, *Tokefield Papers, Old and New*, New York, Doubleday, 1949.

Wells, H. G., *Experiment in Autobiography*, New York, Macmillan, 1934.

Woolf, Virginia, *A Writer's Diary*, London, Hogarth, 1953.

Index